BLOOD
SWEAT&BEERS

DISHES FROM THE KITCHENS OF THE MILESTONE GROUP
MATT BIGLAND, LUKE FRENCH & STACEY SHERWOOD

Blood, Sweat & Beers

First edition printed in 2015 in the UK.

ISBN: 978-1-910863-00-8

Written by: Matt Bigland, Luke French & Stacey Sherwood

Photography by: Paul Cocker

Additional Photography: Stacey Sherwood, Dan Carreras, Luke French

Edited by: Rachel Heward, Carl Reid

Designed by: Paul Cocker, Marc Barker, Phil Turner

Contributors: Kelsie Marsden, Faye Bailey, Sarah Koriba, Kerre Chen, Anna Tebble

me:ze
PUBLISHING

Published by Meze Publishing Limited
Unit 1 Beehive Works
Milton Street
Sheffield S3 7WL
web: www.mezepublishing.co.uk
Tel: 0114 275 7709
Email: info@mezepublishing.co.uk

CONTENTS

INTRODUCTION
MATT & NINA PATEL-BIGLAND

It started with a shell of a building and the desire to create something new in Sheffield where we could express our passion for food, drinks and service. Taking residence in one of Kelham Island's derelict Victorian buildings, nearly ten years ago the area was a relatively unvisited pocket of the city. With a flood submerging the majority of the restaurant just six months after we opened, on the surface it looked like we were destined to fail. But we persevered and this is where it all started: blood, sweat and beers. Before we knew it we were meeting Gordon Ramsey and talking about rearing our own pigs on telly.

From there we developed the ethos that has since become ingrained in the rest of The Milestone Group, but we weren't always so sure of ourselves. When we originally opened we didn't have a strong identity like today. It took two years to find ourselves as we continued to grow, learning a lot of lessons along the journey.

Taking on The Wig & Pen was an opportunity we couldn't miss out on. A city centre gastro pub, this allowed us to offer what we had tried to do at The Milestone alongside everything else, where we had learnt you couldn't be all things to everyone from one venue.

A bigger bar area allowed us to experiment with the wet side of the business, a challenge we found exciting. We sourced craft beers from around the world as well as gins, rums and whiskeys. From there we developed cocktails, which is where our garden to glass idea came from. Growing our own ingredients on the roof top of The Wig & Pen enthused the team and joined the kitchen and front of house together as they worked together on flavours and textures. We had already begun to look for our next project at this point, which would be to grow our own produce to supply our kitchens. This would enable us to expand our ethos in becoming self-sustainable whilst also allowing us to play with new varieties of produce.

The time came when we found the right site, located at Furnace Park, a five minute walk from The Milestone. It was an area of unloved waste land which had been brought to our attention by Sheffield University, who shared our interest in regeneration.

Fast forward seven years and it's blood, sweat and craft beers with December 2014 seeing the opening of our latest venture. A spin off of the original Milestone, where it all started with a pizza and tapas menu. Today we've tweaked it slightly by offering artisan pizzas with toppings inspired by our dishes from The Milestone and The Wig & Pen, including our home grown produce from Furnace Park. In fact we launched Craft & Dough Kelham Island with some of the original pizzas circa 2007 at The Milestone.

We like to keep track of trends, and not just when it comes to the food that we serve. The way people live and work is changing, it's not necessarily that strict nine to five routine anymore. We really wanted this book to reflect that, with a mixture of our favourite recipes for different times of the day or occasions.

We like to get our guests involved too, and love it when they ask us questions about provenance or cooking techniques. This is something that has always happened, especially at The Milestone where the food is often something a little more adventurous or unusual. On Saturday afternoons we found there was a lull in activity so we decided to start up a cookery school. It's about teaching people how to go back to basics and use techniques your grandmother would have used during the war; braising and slow-cooking often discarded or forgotten cuts of meat to get the most flavour out of them, and not wasting a single morsel in the process. It just makes good sense; cook everything fresh, use every cut you can and source as closely to home as possible. That's our ethos.

The genius thing that we did was, we didn't give up.

KICK START
YOUR DAY

Whether you're having your first meal of the day with us or you just need something to get you going, we've developed a few options which will make you wonder why you ever skipped breakfast in the first place. From buttermilk pancakes topped with crispy bacon dripping in maple syrup to a light granola and blackberry dish with sweet cheese, or even a devilishly spicy Bloody Mary; you're sure to find something to blow those cobwebs away.

EGGS BENEDICT

Serves 4

4 English muffins

4 large eggs

150ml chardonnay vinegar

1 banana shallot, finely diced

5 white peppercorns

350g unsalted butter to make
250g beurre noisette

2 egg yolks

5ml sherry vinegar

Table salt

Fresh flat leaf parsley, finely sliced

36 month aged Iberico ham

Place the chardonnay vinegar, shallot and peppercorns in a pan and reduce right down to approximately 10g over a high heat, then set aside to cool.

Place the egg yolks, reduction and 30ml of water in a bowl set over a pan of simmering water and whisk until the yolks become thick and creamy.

To make the beurre noisette, gently heat 350g of unsalted butter until foaming and brown. Strain off the milk solids.

Slowly drizzle in the beurre noisette whilst whisking continuously until it is fully incorporated, then add the sherry vinegar and season with table salt to taste. Set aside until needed.

Place the eggs in a waterbath at 65°c for 45 minutes, then cool in an ice bath immediately.

Bring a pan of water to the boil then remove it from the heat and carefully crack the eggs into it to warm through.

Lightly toast the English muffins and place some Iberico ham on top of them. Carefully peel the shell away from the eggs and place them on top of the ham, then spoon over the hollandaise, followed by a sprinkle of parsley. Serve immediately.

If you do not have a waterbath

If you do not have a vacuum packing machine or waterbath, you can place the ingredients into a zip-lock style bag and bring a pan of water to the desired temperature, then immerse the bag into the water. As long as you maintain the correct temperature you will gain the same results.

SWEET CHEESE,
BLACKBERRIES & GRANOLA

Serves 8

400g full fat cream cheese

Icing sugar

800g blackberry purée

85g glucose syrup

1 lemon, juiced

100g fructose

350ml water

200g rolled porridge oats, sieved

10g table salt

50g maple syrup

20ml vegetable oil

Fresh blackberries for garnish

Blackcurrant leaf oil (see page 151)

Apple marigold leaves

To make the blackberry purée, place 1kg of blackberry in a pan with 150ml water. Bring to a boil, turn off and allow to cool slightly before blending. Pass through a fine sieve and set aside until needed.

Carefully fold the cheese whilst adding the icing sugar until sweetened, then set aside in the fridge in a piping bag.

Take 300g of the blackberry purée and whisk in 80g of icing sugar and pass it through a fine sieve. Then spread it very thinly over greaseproof paper and place in a dehydrator or an oven set to 60°c and dry it out until it becomes brittle. Let it cool and keep it inside an airtight container at room temperature.

Take the remaining 500g of blackberry purée, glucose syrup, fructose and water and place in a pan and slowly bring to the boil. Remove from the heat and stir in the lemon juice then pass through a fine sieve and cool over an ice bath. Churn the mixture to a sorbet in an ice cream machine following the manufacturer's instructions and keep in the freezer until needed.

Place the oats and salt onto an oven tray and drizzle over the vegetable oil and mix them together until they are all coated, then drizzle over the maple syrup and mix again. Place in an oven at 160°c and cook until golden, making sure to stir the oats every 5 minutes to prevent them from sticking to one another. Let the oats cool then keep them in an airtight container at room temperature.

Arrange the preparations delicately in the bowl and serve.

SLOW COOKED DUCK EGG ON TOAST, YORKSHIRE ASPARAGUS AND TRUFFLE BUTTER

Serves 4

4 duck eggs

4 slices of sourdough bread

20 spears of Yorkshire asparagus

200g smoked unsalted butter

1 litre brown chicken stock (see page 153)

130g unsalted butter

200g leeks, white only, finely sliced

190g grated black truffle

125ml Madeira

125ml ruby port

Table salt

1 Paris cap mushroom, finely sliced

Place the chicken stock in a pan and bring to the boil, reduce to 200g in weight then set aside.

Melt 50g of unsalted butter in a new pan, add the leeks and cook over a medium high heat for 5 minutes, stirring constantly so they don't colour at all. Add the reduced brown chicken stock and bring the liquid to a simmer, then add the truffle and simmer for 5 minutes.

Remove the pan from the heat and place the mixture into a blender and blitz to a smooth purée, pass through a fine sieve. Return the purée to a new pan and cook over a low heat. Reduce to 200g in weight making sure you stir it continuously to avoid burning it.

Meanwhile in a new pan add the port and Madeira, cook over a high heat and set the liquid alight to burn off the alcohol, reduce it to a thick syrup then add it to the purée and stir it in.

Remove the pan from the heat and whisk in the remaining 80g of unsalted butter slowly to emulsify it and season with table salt to taste. Immediately place the pan into an ice bath and stir until it is chilled. Transfer to a container and keep in the fridge.

Set a water bath to 62°c and carefully submerge the duck eggs into it. Cook them for 2 hours and then reduce the temperature of the water bath using some ice to 50°c. (Or see non-waterbath method on page 14.)

Meanwhile, trim the asparagus and peel the stalks, then keep them in iced water.

Cut the sourdough into a ring using a large disc cutter, then brush it with a little olive oil and cook it in a dry pan on a very low heat until golden on both sides.

Warm the smoked butter in a pan to 75°c and then place the asparagus spears into it and cook them for 6-8 minutes until tender. Remove from the butter and season with sea salt.

Spread the truffle and butter onto both sides of the toasted sourdough and place it in the bottom of a bowl. Carefully crack the duck egg on to the top of it and season with sea salt, then arrange the asparagus spears and mushroom around the toast and serve.

AMERICAN PANCAKES

Serves 8

650g self-raising flour, sieved

100g caster sugar

8g baking powder

4g bicarbonate of soda

10g table salt

3 large free-range eggs

225ml whole milk

450ml buttermilk

10ml vanilla extract

5ml almond extract

90g unsalted butter, melted

Place all of the ingredients except the butter in an electric mixer using the paddle attachment and mix on a low speed until a smooth batter is formed. Add the butter and make sure it is mixed in thoroughly, then remove from the bowl. Place in a container and cover with cling film, then rest in the fridge for 2 hours.

Heat a large heavy non-stick frying pan over a low heat and add a little unsalted butter, carefully add 75g portions of the batter (add more if you want bigger pancakes!) using a ladle and cook without interfering for a minute or until golden. Then using a palette knife carefully flip the pancake and cook for a further minute. It should be soft and springy to touch.

Serve immediately with some quality maple syrup and crispy smoked Alsace bacon, or with some natural yoghurt, runny honey and compote of summer berries! (See recipe for berry compote on page 154.)

CRABBY EGGS BENEDICT

Serves 4

4 English muffins

4 large eggs

150ml chardonnay vinegar

1 banana shallot, finely diced

5 white peppercorns

300g unsalted butter to make 200g beurre noisette

2 egg yolks

5ml sherry vinegar

Table salt

White pepper

Sea salt

Fresh dill, finely chopped

250g white crab meat, carefully picked to remove any shell

50g brown crab meat, carefully picked to remove any shell

Place the chardonnay vinegar, shallot and peppercorns in a pan and reduce to approximately 10g over a high heat, then set aside to cool.

To make the beurre noisette, gently heat 300g of unsalted butter until foaming and brown. Strain off the milk solids.

Place the egg yolks, reduction and 30ml of water in a bowl set over a pan of simmering water and whisk until the yolks become thick and creamy. Slowly drizzle in the beurre noisette whilst whisking continuously until it is fully incorporated, then add the sherry vinegar and season with table salt to taste, set aside until needed.

Place the eggs in a waterbath at 65°c for 45 minutes, then cool in an ice bath immediately.

(Alternatively use the zip-lock bag method, see page 14.)

Bring a pan of water to the boil then remove it from the heat and carefully crack the eggs into it to warm through.

Combine the crab meat together and season with sea salt and freshly ground white pepper.

Lightly toast the English muffins and add the crab meat on top of them. Carefully peel the shell away from the eggs and place them on top, spoon over the hollandaise, followed by a sprinkle of dill.

Serve immediately.

HENDERSON'S RELISH BLOODY MARY

For the pizza sauce
(use the rest on one of our pizzas)

550g tinned San Marzano tomatoes

15ml extra virgin olive oil

10g table salt

15g basil leaves

15g oregano leaves

50ml vodka

2 soup spoons pizza sauce

4 drops sriracha chilli sauce

4 dashes Henderson's Relish

25ml lemon juice

Pinch salt

Pinch cracked black pepper

2 basil leaves

To make the pizza sauce, place all of the ingredients in a tall container and use a stick blender to pulse the mixture to combine. Make sure you don't completely purée it because if you blend too many tomato seeds into the sauce, it will become bitter.

To make the Bloody Mary, place all ingredients into a cocktail glass over ice. Roll the cocktail glass and tin gently for 1 minute. Do not shake, rolling the drink allows the cracked pepper and tomato sauce to mix without making the tomato sauce foamy and diluted. Pour into a glass with fresh ice and garnish with 2 sip straws, sprig of basil and tiny pinch of black pepper. Add some slices of tomato, cucumber or celery if you like!

Best served in a Collins glass.

A LIGHT BITE

Perfect as starters, sharers or snacks, these dishes stand up on their own as delicate tasters of what we have on our menus, or are a great way to whet your appetite before a main course. Think goats' cheese and beetroot, heritage tomatoes or a classic Caesar salad. This is also an opportunity to experiment with something new; the crab and cucumber jelly is an interesting approach to this classic combination, or why not try your hand at the duck heart recipe? One of the hardest working muscles, they are wonderfully succulent and are fantastic value for money, being an often neglected part of the bird.

CHARRED HISPI CABBAGE, ALMOND PESTO AND SMOKED BACON

Serves 4

1 hispi cabbage, quartered

80g watercress

1 garlic clove, peeled and smashed

50g Parmesan, finely grated

50g flaked almonds, toasted

50ml extra virgin olive oil

15ml lemon juice

10g caster sugar

Table salt

Pancetta slices

Vegetable oil for frying

Place all of the ingredients except the salt, cabbage and pancetta in a food processor and blend until a course textured pesto is achieved, season with salt to taste and set aside.

Place the pancetta slices on a heavy baking sheet lined with greaseproof paper, then cook in the oven at 180°c until golden and crispy, then drain off the excess fat on kitchen paper and leave to cool.

Heat a large non stick frying pan and add a little vegetable oil, then place the cabbage hearts flat side down and caramelise heavily on both sides. Remove from the pan and place on a tray and spoon over the almond pesto, then break up the crispy pancetta and sprinkle it on top of the pesto.

CELERIAC AND APPLE SOUP, SAGE AND YORKSHIRE BLUE

Serves 8

50ml extra virgin olive oil

2 large white onions, finely sliced

1 celery stalk, finely sliced

1 head of celeriac, peeled and finely sliced

4 Cox's apples, cored and quartered

10g thyme leaves

2 litres vegetable stock (see page 155)

Table salt

Sage leaves

Yorkshire blue cheese, crumbled

1 Granny Smith apple, cut into 5mm dice

Onion oil (see page 151)

Heat the oil in a heavy based pan then add the onions and celery and cook over a medium heat whilst stirring regularly for 10 minutes until soft. Add the celeriac, Cox's apples and thyme leaves and cook for 3 minutes. Then add the stock and simmer over a low heat for 30 minutes until the celeriac is tender.

Remove the pan from the heat and purée the mixture with a blender until smooth, then pass through a fine mesh sieve and season with table salt to taste.

Deep fry the sage leaves in vegetable oil at 180°c until crispy, then drain on kitchen paper and season with sea salt.

Combine the Granny Smith apple, cheese and sage then serve with the soup and a little onion oil.

TUNNEL
TOMATO SALAD

Serves 4.

Heritage tomatoes, washed and cut into various shapes and sizes

250ml Bloody Mary (see page 24)

2.5g agar agar, available from most good supermarkets and health shops

1 ball of buffalo mozzarella

5 bulbs of maple wood smoked garlic, peeled

200ml extra virgin olive oil

Table salt

Sea salt

Garden leaves and herbs

1 banana shallot, peeled and thinly sliced into rings

100ml pickling liquor (see page 149)

Freeze dried tomato powder, optional

Onion oil (see page 151)

Black pepper

Cover the shallot rings with the pickling liquor and leave them for 24 hours in the fridge. Alternatively use a vacuum packer and you can use them immediately.

Slice some of the tomatoes so they are 3mm thick, then place them on a sheet of greaseproof paper and then onto a dehydrator tray or an ovenproof tray. Drizzle over a little olive oil, sea salt and a little freshly ground black pepper and place in the oven or dehydrator set to 60°c until some of them are chewy and leave some to go brittle. Let them cool and store in an airtight container at room temperature until needed.

Place the smoked garlic cloves with the olive oil and 10g of table salt into a pan with a lid and cook in an oven at 100°c until they are soft then strain the oil off and reserve it, blend the garlic until smooth and pass through a fine sieve, chill until needed.

Warm the Bloody Mary very gently to 90°c and then gradually whisk in the agar. Whisk gently for 3 minutes then pass through a fine sieve into a shallow container lined with a double layer of cling film. Leave to set in the fridge and then cut into 1cm cubes when set and keep chilled until needed.

Season the tomatoes with a little sea salt and paint a little of the smoked garlic purée onto some of them at random.

Tear up the mozzarella, season it with sea salt and marinate it in a little onion oil for a short while.

Arrange the tomatoes, herbs, tomato powder, Bloody Mary jelly and onion oil on a plate and serve.

GOATS' CHEESE, CHERRY BLACKCURRANT & BEETROOT

Serves 4

100g Yorkshire goats' cheese, whipped (see page 46)

1 large red beetroot, washed

100g dried cherries

Freeze-dried cherries, optional

100ml pickling liquor (see page 149)

Blackcurrant leaf oil (see page151)

800g blackcurrant purée

85g glucose syrup

100g fructose

80g icing sugar

1 lemon, juiced

350ml water

Sea salt

Garden leaves

To make the blackcurrant purée, place 1kg of blackcurrants in a pan with 150ml water. Bring to a boil, turn off and allow to cool slightly before blending. Pass through a fine sieve and set aside until needed.

Bring the pickling liquor to the boil then pour it over the dried cherries and cover tightly with cling film. Leave for 1 hour at room temperature then keep chilled.

Take 300g of the blackcurrant purée, whisk in the icing sugar and pass it through a fine sieve. Then spread it very thinly over greaseproof paper and place in a dehydrator or an oven set to 60°c. Dry it out until it becomes brittle, then let it cool and keep it inside an airtight container at room temperature.

Take the remaining 500g of blackcurrant purée, glucose syrup, fructose and water and place in a pan. Slowly bring to the boil, remove from the heat and stir in the lemon juice, then pass through a fine sieve and cool over a bowl of ice. Churn the mixture to a sorbet in an ice cream machine following the manufacturer's instructions and keep in the freezer until needed.

Just before serving, slice the beetroot (ideally with a mandoline if you have one) to a thickness no more than 2mm and season with sea salt.

Pipe the goats' cheese on to the centre of the plate, sprinkle with the freeze-dried cherries, arrange the sliced beetroot, pickled cherries and garden leaves around the plate. Add a spoonfull of the blackcurrant sorbet on top of the freeze-dried cherries and dress the plate with a little blackcurrant leaf oil.

SHRIVELLED CARROTS, SPICED SHERBET, PINE, FENNEL & BLACKCURRANT LEAF

Serves 4

16 carrots,
peeled to 50g each in weight

300ml carrot juice

350g caster sugar

10g liquorice concentrate

4g table salt

Citric acid powder

2 teaspoons of mixed spice

Zest of 1 lemon

30g maple syrup

15ml blackcurrant leaf oil (see page 151)

15ml pine vinegar (see page 152)

Sugar coated fennel seeds

Fennel fronds

Place the carrot juice, salt and 150g of caster sugar in a pan and gently heat to dissolve, then bring to the boil, add the liquorice concentrate and remove from the heat and pass through a fine sieve over an ice bath (a bowl of water and ice) to chill.

Place the chilled carrot and liquorice syrup in a vacuum bag with the carrots and seal on full pressure, place in a water bath or pan of water heated to 88°c and cook until they are tender.

(Alternatively use the zip-lock bag method, see page 14.)

Remove the bags from the water and let them cool naturally. Once cool, remove the carrots from the syrup and place them on a sheet of greaseproof paper on a tray and dehydrate them in an oven at 60°c until they have shrivelled and have a chewy and leathery texture. Remove from the oven and let them cool naturally, keep in an airtight container at room temperature until needed.

Combine the maple syrup, pine vinegar and blackcurrant leaf oil and whisk well. Set aside in the fridge until needed.

To make the spiced sherbet, place 200g of caster sugar in a blender with the lemon zest and mixed spice and blend until fully combined, add a little citric acid at a time until the desired sourness is achieved. Store in an airtight container at room temperature until needed.

Place the carrots in a bowl and toss them with a little of the pine and blackcurrant leaf oil dressing, then roll them in the spiced sherbet and arrange on a plate. Sprinkle some of the fennel seeds on to each carrot and then some fresh fennel fronds. Drizzle a little more of the dressing around the carrots and serve immediately.

SALAD OF TORCHED MACKEREL, KING SCALLOP AND SPECK

Serves 4

4 large king scallops

Extra virgin olive oil

4 fillets of mackerel, boneless

40g table salt

40g caster sugar

200g water

Sea salt

25g samphire, blanched in salted boiling water for 5 seconds and refreshed in iced water

1 small banana shallot, peeled and very thinly sliced

25g cucumber flesh, thinly sliced

25g asparagus, thinly sliced

1 slice of prosciutto di speck

A selection of garden herbs, flowers and leaves

Lumpfish roe

Crème fraîche

Place the table salt, water and caster sugar in a pan and bring to the boil so they dissolve, then chill completely. When chilled, submerge the mackerel fillet into the liquid and leave at room temperature for 20 minutes.

After 20 minutes, carefully pour away and discard the liquid and leave the mackerel fillet to rinse under cold running water for 5 minutes, then pat dry carefully with kitchen paper and set aside until needed.

Cut each mackerel fillet into 3 pieces and rub each piece with a little olive oil, then torch it with a propane powered blow torch until blackened and set aside. (If you do not have a blow torch place under a very hot grill until the skin is blackened.)

Heat a non-stick frying pan until smoking then add a drop of olive oil and carefully place the scallop in the pan. Leave it for 30 seconds and then turn it over and leave it for a further 30 seconds. Remove from the pan and rest on kitchen paper whilst you prepare the rest of the ingredients.

Arrange attractively on a plate and serve immediately.

CAESAR SALAD

Serves 4. The egg yolks need to cure 4 weeks in advance.

65g garlic cloves, halved and hearts removed

50g pickled white anchovies

10ml lemon juice

30ml water

25ml extra virgin olive oil

15g Dijon mustard

Semi-skimmed milk

75g Parmesan

Table salt

Caster sugar

4 duck egg yolks

1 large little gem lettuce, washed and cut into quarters

20g panko breadcrumbs, toasted

36 month aged Iberico ham, finely sliced

Onion oil (see page 151)

Fresh white anchovies, to garnish

Combine 100g of table salt and 100g of caster sugar. Place half of it in the bottom of a small tray and then place the duck egg yolks on top and cover them with the remaining salt and sugar mixture. Cover with cling film and leave at room temperature for 7 days to cure.

Remove the egg yolks from the cure and rinse them under cold water carefully, then pat them dry with kitchen paper and wrap in cheesecloth. Hang them in your refrigerator for 3 weeks or until completely dry, then store in an airtight container until needed. Alternatively just use some boiled egg yolks.

Place the garlic in a pan and cover it with milk, slowly bring to a boil and drain off the milk. Repeat this process 5 more times then place the garlic in a pan with 300ml of fresh milk and simmer them together over a low heat until the milk has reduced by half, stirring occasionally. Transfer to a blender and blend to a smooth purée.

Add the anchovies, mustard, Parmesan, water and lemon juice and blend again, gradually add the olive oil and remove from the blender, chill and set aside until needed.

Drizzle the lettuce with the dressing, followed by the ham, top with the breadcrumbs and some fresh anchovies, and then grate over the duck egg yolks and more fresh Parmesan. Season and then drizzle with onion oil before serving.

TORCHED MACKEREL WITH PONZU

Serves 4

4 large fillets of mackerel

250ml water

15g table salt

35g golden caster sugar

8 pink peppercorns

2 vanilla pods, split

Ponzu (see page 147)

20g wild rice

Onion oil (see page 151)

A selection of coriander and fennel shoots

Place the water, sugar, salt, peppercorns and vanilla pods into a pan and gently bring to the boil, remove from the heat and let it cool naturally. Chill completely in the fridge.

Place a small pan of vegetable oil on a medium high heat, take it to a temperature of 220°c, then carefully submerge the wild rice into the hot oil, as soon as the rice begins to puff up, remove immediately and drain on kitchen paper. Whilst still hot season the rice with an equal mix of table salt and caster sugar then set aside until needed.

Carefully remove any bones from the mackerel, then gently wash it under cold running water and submerge it into the brine. Leave it in the brine for 25 minutes then remove it and gently wash it again under cold running water for 1 minute. Pat the mackerel dry using kitchen paper.

Carefully remove the membrane from on top of the skin of the mackerel using a pair of tweezers, if you get it right the first time it should come off in one piece.

Using a sharp knife, trim the mackerel to the shape you want then place it on a tray lightly greased with olive oil skin side up.

Using a propane-powered blow torch, carefully run the flame across the skin side of the fish until it is golden all over and begins to blacken in some areas, or place under a very high grill until blackened.

Place a spoon of the ponzu in the bottom of a bowl, drizzle over a little onion oil and place the mackerel to the side of it and garnish the bowl with the herbs and puffed rice.

DUCK HEARTS, CELERIAC, YORKSHIRE BLUE AND PORT

Serves 4

12 duck hearts, sinew removed

Celeriac purée (see recipe for beef cheek on page 107)

50g Yorkshire blue cheese, at room temperature

For the Port reduction

500ml Ruby Port

100g caster sugar

1 star anise

4 sprigs of thyme

2 vanilla pods

Pinch of Table salt

Pickled cherries (see recipe for beets, blackcurrant and cherries on page 34)

For the Granola

200g rolled porridge oats, sieved

Table salt

50g maple syrup

20ml vegetable oil

Sea salt

Vegetable oil

Unsalted butter

2 sprigs of fresh thyme

2 garlic cloves, peeled and smashed

Onion oil (see page 151)

1 large slice of celeriac, 1cm thick

50g smoked unsalted butter

8 button onions, halved and charred

Place the slice of celeriac, smoked butter and a good pinch of table salt into a vacuum bag and cook in a waterbath at 88°c until tender, then cool in an ice bath immediately.

(Alternatively use the zip-lock bag method, see page 14.)

To make a Port reduction, add the Port, caster sugar, star anise, thyme and vanilla pods to a pan and reduce by at least half on a high heat until a thick syrup consistency. Allow to cool then taste and season with salt as needed.

Slice the celeriac into small triangles.

Warm the celeriac purée gently in a saucepan.

Gently fry the celeriac slices in a dry pan until caramelised and set aside.

To make the granola, place the oats and salt onto an oven tray and drizzle over the vegetable oil and mix them together until they are all coated, then drizzle over the maple syrup and mix again. Place in an oven at 160°c and cook until golden, making sure to stir the oats every 5 minutes to prevent them from sticking to one another. Let the oats cool then keep them in an airtight container at room temperature.

Heat a frying pan over a high heat and add a little vegetable oil, season the duck hearts with table salt and carefully place in the pan, quickly brown them all over and add a tablespoon of butter. When the butter is foaming add garlic and thyme and quickly baste the hearts with the garlic and thyme infused butter. Immediately remove from the pan and rest on kitchen paper.

Arrange on a plate with the onions, celeriac, port reduction, granola, pickled cherries, cheese and purée and serve immediately.

WHIPPED GOATS' CHEESE, PICKLED BEETROOT AND BEETROOT KETCHUP

Serves 4

125g mascarpone

250g goats' cheese

10ml white truffle oil

Table salt

150ml pickling liquor (see page 149)

1 large red beetroot

1 large golden beetroot

1 large striped beetroot

250ml beetroot juice

1.35g agar agar

1 small banana shallot, finely diced

75ml chardonnay vinegar

100g caster sugar

Onion oil (see page 151)

Bitter salad leaves and herbs, to garnish

Place the mascarpone, goats' cheese, 2.5g table salt and the truffle oil into a Thermomix and set the temperature to 80°c on speed 5 for 5 minutes. After 5 minutes increase the speed to setting 10 for 2 minutes. Remove the mixture and place it in to a piping bag, then tie it and let it cool naturally. Keep it in the fridge. (Alternatively you can warm the mascarpone in a bowl set over a pan of simmering water and whisk in the goats' cheese a little at a time until fully incorporated.)

Place the beetroot juice and 2.5g table salt in to a clean Thermomix jug and set the temperature to 90°c on speed 4. When it reaches 90°c add the agar agar and blend on high speed for 1 minute. (Alternatively use the method for the goat's cheese and Henderson's pizza on page 95.)

Pour it through a fine sieve into a clean container over an ice bath and leave it until it is completely cool and has set. Return the mixture to a blender and blitz until it is a smooth gel, then pass through a fine sieve into a clean bowl.

Place the vinegar and sugar in a pan and bring to the boil. Remove from the heat and chill completely. When chilled, place the liquid and the shallot in a vacuum bag and seal at full pressure and leave it for 10 minutes.

(Alternatively use the zip-lock bag method, see page 14.)

Stir the shallot liquid into the beetroot gel until they are combined completely and keep in the fridge.

Slice the beetroots to a thickness of 3mm (ideally using a mandoline) and reserve the same coloured beetroots together in iced water until they are all sliced.

Cut 50g of the sliced red beetroot into cubes and fold it through the beetroot gel.

Using a disc cutter, cut the rest of the sliced beetroot into circles. Waste as little as possible by using the largest ring cutters possible for each slice. Place the discs of the same coloured beetroot into vacuum bags with 50ml of pickling liquor per bag and seal at full pressure then keep in the fridge.

(Alternatively use the zip-lock bag method, see page 14.)

Remove the whipped goats' cheese from the fridge and let it come to room temperature. Pipe it on to a plate with a spoon of beetroot ketchup and onion oil.

Remove the beetroot discs from the pickling liquor and pat dry using kitchen paper, then arrange them over the cheese.

Garnish the plate with a selection of seasonal bitter salad leaves and herbs.

CRAB AND CUCUMBER

Serves 8

570ml filtered cucumber juice

Chardonnay vinegar

Table salt

3 sheets of gold leaf gelatine

100g fresh white crab meat, carefully picked to remove all shell

1 cucumber

300g fresh dill, blanched in boiling water then refreshed in ice, squeezed dry

Vegetable oil

Crème fraîche

Caster sugar

Fresh horseradish, finely grated

Sea salt

Dried Wakame seaweed, ground to a powder

Fennel fronds

Smoked trout roe

Lumpfish roe

Borage flowers

Samphire

Lemon juice

Blend the dill with double its weight in vegetable oil and 10% of the total weight in table salt until it reaches 80°c then pass it through a fine sieve over an ice bath and keep in a cool dark place until needed.

Place the gelatine in cold water and let it sit for a few minutes until soft. This process is called blooming, which softens the gelatine.

Warm 190ml of the cucumber juice to 70°c and then remove from the heat and stir in the gelatine. Then stir in the remaining cucumber juice and season with table salt and chardonnay vinegar until it has a delicate pickled flavour. Pass through a fine sieve and chill in your desired bowls over ice until set. Then cover and place in the fridge until needed.

Add the horseradish to the crème fraiche until it has the desired heat and then season with a little caster sugar, table salt and chardonnay vinegar. Set aside in the fridge until needed.

Cut the skin away from the cucumber and slice into 5mm thick lengths then cut into 5mm dice, place the cucumber in a vacuum bag and seal at full pressure. Repeat this process 5 times then set aside in the fridge (alternatively just use fresh cucumber.)

Place the crab meat in a bowl and season with a little sea salt and black pepper and a little lemon juice to taste.

Remove the jelly from the fridge and arrange the wakame seaweed, fennel fronds, smoked trout roe, lumpfish roe, borage flowers and samphire on top of with a squeeze of lemon juice and serve.

OUR COOKING ETHOS
LUKE FRENCH

While the style of the food, and the venues themselves, often differ greatly within The Milestone Group, the principles are the same throughout. The quality of ingredients and the time, effort and care put into creating dishes is consistent at each place. Knowledgeable and passionate, our staff always strive to offer excellent service from the kitchen all the way through to front of house.

The Milestone is a gastropub at the end of the day, but we're not just doing the norm. We don't do things for the sake of it; there's no point making a dish look amazing if it doesn't taste so. We aim to use our ingredients in the most interesting way possible and when you strip it down it's simple cooking, but it's about what you do with the visual. For example take one ingredient, and use it to serve several purposes - preserve it, pickle it, purée it and manipulate the way it looks and tastes to offer that wow factor. Keep the number of ingredients simple but play with the way they come across and get people eating with their eyes too.

I read a lot of cook books and was definitely inspired by the people I learnt from, but more often than not I take inspiration from nature, especially when it comes to presentation and choice of ingredients. Every time I go to our Furnace Park allotment I come back with ideas. From planting a seed to the end of a plant's life we can develop ideas and can use it

each step of the way in various forms. To keep track of all of this I write notes constantly, and refer back to them when it's menu planning time.

When we come up with menus, across the company, we all sit down together and talk about what everyone likes, refine the ideas and work out what's in season and how we can make the best of it. There are patterns of ingredients and classic combinations that work well, and if it's not broken, then why fix it? Instead we look to enhance traditional pairings, and find exciting innovative ways of using them. An example of this is the goats' cheese and beetroot starter. A fantastic combination, the dish started out simply as the cheese crumbled over the vegetable. We then developed it by experimenting with whipping the cheese in a Thermomix, which created a creamy melt in the mouth texture and added depth to the beetroot by pickling some and creating a ketchup out of the excess. This enabled us to shape the way it looks and build it up visually as well as in taste and texture. Finish with some fresh micro herbs from the garden and you've got something spectacular. But even then the evolution of the dish hasn't stopped – different types of beetroot grow in different seasons, meaning it will vary in colour and flavour depending on when you are eating it. I think this idea of never settling on a 'finished' dish and working with the ingredients throughout the year means we are always creating food that really stands out from the crowd.

To maintain this philosophy, we keep our own allotment of various plants, flowers, herbs and vegetables and even use the space on the roof of The Milestone to grow. And instead of pansies, we grow tomatoes in hanging baskets and pots outside The Wig and Pen, so every inch of space is utilised. All of the chefs are involved in the process, helping to plant, maintain and harvest the allotment. We also all go out foraging for things like hedgerow berries and wild roses, taking the opportunity to pick everything whether it can be used immediately or not. Nothing is wasted, and many such ingredients can be used in pickles, oils or dressings.

And this extends across the whole company. For instance if a fresh crop of something is grown then it will be preserved or infused and used as part of a starter at The Milestone, as a topping on a pizza at Craft & Dough or stirred into a risotto at The Wig and Pen. We also work many of our own fruits and herbs into our cocktails. We'll take one ingredient and use it in a variety of ways, adapting it to suit the style of each venue.

Where we can't grow our own, we source locally. The food miles are kept down by making the most of growers in Yorkshire and Derbyshire, and the same can be said of our meat, game and fish.

If you're unsure about where to get some of the ingredients in this book from, then we'd advise to shop local. Find your nearest greengrocers or allotment – many people grow more than enough for themselves and are willing to sell at very reasonable prices. For some of the micro herbs and more unusual ingredients, you can source online or we'd encourage you to try growing it yourself. Nothing we use is particularly hard to get hold of and a lot of it grows naturally, so get foraging!

COMFORT FOOD

This is the stuff you turn to when you're in need of a bit of TLC. Combining nostalgia and tradition with more unusual cooking techniques, your old favourites are given a new lease of life here. There's classic sausage and mash, the best roast chicken that'll ever grace your dining room table and a cauliflower cheese recipe that does away with the gloopy mess but retains all of the flavour. And if it's a party or picnic you're catering for, steer clear from the supermarket and whip up your own sausage roll and scotch eggs. Trust us, you'll never go back.

LEMON AND THYME ROAST CHICKEN WITH TEWKESBURY MUSTARD SAUCE

Serves 2

1 x 2kg free-range chicken

5 litres cold water

400g table salt

2 lemons

50g thyme

10 chicken wings

1 carrot, peeled and sliced into 2cm pieces

1 white onion, peeled and finely sliced

4 cloves of garlic, smashed

20g Tewkesbury mustard

1 tsp tarragon leaves, chopped

250ml white wine

300ml brown chicken stock (see page 153)

100g unsalted butter, softened

Sea salt

Vegetable oil

Make sure the chicken is completely free from trussing, remove the wing tips and keep them with the chicken wings. Whisk the salt into the water until dissolved to make a brine. Place the chicken in a large container and then pour the brine over the top and place in the fridge for 12 hours.

Remove the chicken from the brine and pat dry.

Soften the lemons by rolling them on a work surface and then prick them a few times with a small knife. Place the lemons and the thyme inside the cavity of the chicken.

Rub the butter all over the chicken and then season it generously all over with sea salt. Place the chicken in a roasting tray with the chicken wings and tips, carrots and garlic.

Place the chicken in an oven heated to 90°c and cook until the core temperature of the breast reaches 62°c.

Remove the chicken from the oven and place it on a wire cooling rack set over a new tray and let it rest for 20 minutes. Set the roasting tray aside.

Meanwhile turn the oven up to 240°c, place a heavy based pan over a high heat and add a little vegetable oil. When the oil is hot add the sliced onion and cook over a high heat until heavily caramelised and almost burnt. Then remove them from the pan and repeat this process with the contents of the roasting tray from the chicken.

Add the onion back to the pan and then deglaze it with the white wine and reduce it by half. Then add the brown chicken stock and simmer for 5 minutes. Add the juices from the chicken now it has rested then pass the sauce through a fine sieve into a clean pan and whisk in the mustard and stir in the tarragon.

Return the chicken to the hot oven until golden and crispy all over (around 10 minutes) remove from the oven, and rest.

Serve the chicken with the roasted lemons from the cavity of bird, mustard sauce, roasted potatoes and some steamed seasonal greens.

BEEF SHORT RIB, POTATO & MUSHROOMS

Serves 4. This dish takes 3 days to prepare.

4 beef short ribs

50g dried ceps

50g cep powder

Vegetable oil

Table salt

2 chestnut mushrooms

4 button mushrooms

50ml mushroom oil (see page 151)

1kg waxy potatoes, peeled

240ml whole milk, warmed to 80°c

250g unsalted butter

Grapeseed oil

100g mushroom reduction (see page 102)

20g mushroom oil (see page 151)

100g pickled Shimeji mushrooms (see page 102)

Carefully trim the ribs of any sinew from the meat and bones then heavily brown off in a hot pan with a little vegetable oil.

Place in a vacuum bag and cook in a water bath at 65° for 72 hours. After cooking plunge into an ice bath to chill immediately. (Alternatively use the method on page 14.)

Remove the ribs from the bag and pat dry with kitchen paper.

Trim the meat in to neat pieces and re-seal in a new vacuum bag and keep chilled. Reserve the bones; give them a good clean as you can use these for presentation.

Heat a pan of water to 80°c.

Slice the potatoes into 1cm thick pieces and rinse for 5 minutes under cold running water. Place them in the pan of water and cook them for 30 minutes. Drain off the potatoes then rinse them under cold running water once again.

Bring a new pan of salted water to the boil and add the potatoes, cook them until extremely soft and they are falling apart.

Drain the potatoes and place them in a clean pan over a very low heat to dry them out, stirring regularly. Pass the potatoes through a ricer (or alternatively mash) over 250g of butter and mix together, then pass the mixture through a fine sieve and gradually add the warmed milk and table salt to taste. Keep warm and set aside.

Slice the mushrooms very thinly (ideally using a mandoline) and set aside.

Heat a water bath to 65°c and place the portioned rib meat in to heat up to temperature. When the core temperature of 65°c is reached, remove the meat from the bath and let it rest in the bag for 10 minutes.

Combine the mushroom reduction and mushroom oil, whisk them together forming an extremely rich mushroom sauce.

Remove the meat from the bag, dry it with some kitchen paper and seal it in a hot pan with a little grapeseed oil until brown on all sides, then rest it for a further 5 minutes.

Arrange some of the potato purée on a plate then the rib bone then place a piece of the rib meat on top. Add the mushrooms and the mushroom sauce and serve.

CAULIFLOWER CHEESE, HENDERSON'S RELISH KETCHUP

Serves 4

1 cauliflower

180g Parmesan, blitzed to fine powder

375ml vegetable stock (see page 155)

300ml semi-skimmed milk

2 tsp English mustard

2 tsp tapioca starch

320g unsalted butter

2 tbsp plain flour

125g finely grated Gruyère cheese

250ml chicken stock, reduced to 25ml

250ml Gewurztraminer wine, reduced to 25ml

150ml double cream

Table salt

3 tsp sherry vinegar

Bunch of fresh thyme

Henderson's Relish ketchup (see page 95)

Heat the vegetable stock to 90°c and stir in the Parmesan, then cover and infuse the mixture for 20 minutes.

Pass the mixture through a fine sieve and place in a clean pan with the milk, English mustard and tapioca, then blitz with a handheld blender and heat the mixture to 85°c.

Melt 70g of butter in a new pan and then stir in the flour and cook to make a roux, stirring constantly until foaming over a medium heat. Then gradually add the Parmesan mixture, stirring constantly.

Reduce the heat and gently cook the mixture for 15 minutes.

Add the Gruyère and stir until it has completely melted, then add the cream, reduced wine and chicken stock, a teaspoon of table salt and sherry vinegar. Then pass through a fine sieve and transfer to a piping bag and keep warm until needed.

Slice through the whole cauliflower so you have a cross section approximately 4cm thick.

Place the remaining butter in a heavy based pan and melt it over a medium high heat until it begins to foam, then add 10g of table salt and the slice of cauliflower and reduce the heat.

Continuously baste the cauliflower with the foaming butter over a low heat until it has heavily caramelised and is almost falling apart, then add the thyme and baste again for 1 minute.

Immediately remove the slice of cauliflower very carefully using a fish slice and drain off any excess butter.

Arrange the cauliflower on the plate with the cheese sauce and Henderson's Relish ketchup.

APPLE & PORK SAUSAGE ROLL, BLOODY MARY KETCHUP

Serves 4

Bloody Mary jelly (see recipe for tunnel tomato salad on page 32)
2 tbsp sea salt
1 tsp ground white pepper
½ tsp grated nutmeg
½ tsp ground mace
1 tsp ground coriander
700g pork shoulder, minced
300g pork belly, minced
100g panko breadcrumbs
1 tsp finely chopped fresh sage
2 Granny Smith apples, finely diced
1 free-range egg
Puff pastry

Mix the mince meat with the salt, spices, breadcrumbs, sage, diced apple and 100g cold water until evenly blended then set aside.

Blitz the egg using a hand held blender and set aside.

Purée the Bloody Mary jelly using a blender and pass through a fine sieve and set aside in the fridge until needed.

Roll out the puff pastry and then work the sausage meat into a long, even roll and place along the length of the pastry. Brush the exposed pastry with beaten egg, then roll over, crimp the join and brush the pastry with the egg wash.

Place the roll on a heavy baking sheet and bake at 180°c until golden brown and cooked through.

Slice and serve with the spicy ketchup.

FISH AND CHIPS, PEAS, TARTARE SAUCE AND PICKLED LEMON

Serves 4

Beer batter (see page 156)

4 skinless halibut fillets, approximately 160g each

8 large floury potatoes

Mayonnaise (see page 148)

1 large duck egg egg, hardboiled, shelled and finely grated

Handful of flat leaf parsley, finely chopped

2 tbsp capers, finely chopped

3 tbsp gherkins, finely chopped

2 large banana shallots, peeled and finely chopped

30g unsalted butter

125ml brown chicken stock

1 tsp mint, finely chopped

300g frozen peas

Sea salt

Table salt

Chardonnay vinegar

Grapeseed oil

Caster sugar

Pickled lemon slices (see page 149)

Peel the potatoes and cut them in to chips 2x2cm thick. Rinse them under cold running water for 10 minutes.

Fill a pan with cold water and add 10% of the water's weight in table salt and whisk together to dissolve. Add the chips and gently bring to a boil. Boil them until they are soft and almost falling apart, then immediately remove them from the water and place them on a wire cooling rack. Place the rack on a baking sheet and put them in the freezer for 1 hour.

Bring the grapeseed oil in a deep fryer to 140°c then blanch the chips in the oil until the oil stops bubbling and they almost start to colour. Then remove them from the oil and drain them on kitchen paper and set aside in the fridge.

Place the mayonnaise in a bowl and add the egg, gherkins, capers, parsley, and one diced banana shallot. Gently stir the ingredients together, then season with table salt to taste and set aside in the fridge.

Place a saucepan over a low heat and add the butter, the remaining diced banana shallot and a pinch of table salt and cook until soft and without colour, stirring occasionally. Add the brown chicken stock and mint then bring the mixture to a boil. Add the peas and simmer for 5 minutes. Remove the pan from the heat and place the mixture into a blender and blitz to a smooth purée. Then season with a little chardonnay vinegar, table salt and caster sugar to taste, pass through a fine sieve and set aside.

Increase the heat of the oil to 180°c and then cook the chips one last time until golden brown and crispy. Drain them on kitchen paper and season with a little sea salt and set aside.

Dip the halibut fillets into the batter and drain off any excess then carefully place them into the 180°c oil and cook them for 4-5 minutes until crispy and golden all over. Remove them from the oil and drain them on kitchen paper and season with sea salt.

Serve with the pea purée, a spoon of the tartare sauce beside it, stack the chips up and place the fish next to them. Arrange the pickled lemon slices on the plate and serve.

SCOTCH EGGS AND HENDERSON'S RELISH KETCHUP

Serves 4

For the Henderson's Relish ketchup

125ml Henderson's Relish

1.35g agar agar (available in good supermarkets and health food shops)

600g sausage meat

1 tsp freshly ground black pepper

1 tsp cayenne pepper

12 quail eggs, refrigerated

Plain flour

1 egg, beaten

150g panko breadcrumbs

For the Henderson's ketchup, place the Henderson's Relish in to a small saucepan and bring to the boil, then gradually whisk in the agar agar and lower the heat to a simmer. Continuously whisk the liquid for 2 minutes and then immediately pour through a fine sieve over an ice bath (a bowl of water and ice) and leave until it is cold and set.

Combine the sausage meat, cayenne and black pepper.

Bring a large pan of water to the boil, then carefully place the quail eggs into it and boil for 2 minutes then immediately plunge them into an ice bath (a bowl of ice and water) to chill.

When the eggs have chilled, peel off the shells and set aside.

Roll 50g of sausage meat into a ball and then flatten it into a cylindrical shape big enough to wrap around the peeled egg, then place it onto a piece of cling film.

Wrap the meat around the egg using the cling film to help you maintain the shape and press the edges together to seal, making sure not to squash the egg inside of the sausage meat.

Roll the balls into a bowl of plain flour and dust off any excess, then into a bowl with the beaten egg, and then finally into a bowl with the breadcrumbs. Repeat this process until all of the balls are coated. Place them in the fridge for 1 hour.

Deep fry the scotch eggs at 180°c for 2 minutes then place the eggs on a cooling rack and place in the oven at 180°c for 4 minutes.

Serve with the Henderson's Relish ketchup.

SAUSAGES & MASH

Serves 4

8 good quality pork sausages from your local butcher

4 tbsp red onion marmalade (see page 156)

1 litre brown chicken stock (see page 153)

25g unsalted butter

150ml port

150ml Madeira

150ml white wine

1 tsp ground Chinese five-spice

2 sprigs thyme (leaves only), chopped

2 large banana shallots, finely sliced

2 cloves of garlic, sliced

20ml sherry vinegar

50g smoked pancetta, sliced

1kg waxy potatoes, peeled

240ml whole milk, warmed to 80°c

250g unsalted butter

Onion oil (see page 151)

5 button onions

Table salt to taste

Vegetable oil

Heat 25g of butter in a heavy based saucepan and add the shallots, cook for 5 minutes over a low heat until they are soft and translucent. Add the garlic, thyme and five-spice and cook out for a further 5 minutes, stirring regularly.

Deglaze the pan with the sherry vinegar and cook out until it has all evaporated, then add the white wine and reduce by two thirds, repeat this process with the Madeira and finally the port.

Add the chicken stock and pancetta and then gently reduce the sauce by two thirds again, then pass through a fine sieve and set aside.

Heat a pan of water to 80°c.

Slice the potatoes into 1cm thick pieces and rinse for 5 minutes under cold running water. Place them in the pan of water and cook them for 30 minutes. Drain off the potatoes then rinse them under cold running water once again.

Bring a new pan of salted water to the boil and add the potatoes, cook them until extremely soft and they are falling apart.

Drain the potatoes and place them in a clean pan over a very low heat to dry them out, stirring regularly. Pass the potatoes through a ricer (or alternatively mash) over 250g of butter and mix together, then pass the mixture through a fine sieve and gradually add the warmed milk and table salt to taste. Transfer to a piping bag, keep warm and set aside until needed.

Peel the button onions and char in a hot pan with a little vegetable oil until blackened then peel each layer away and set aside.

Place a little vegetable oil in an oven proof pan and place it over a gentle heat, add the sausages and cook them whilst turning regularly until they begin to caramelise all over, then transfer the pan to an oven heated to 175°c and cook for a further 10 minutes. Remove the pan from the oven and remove the sausages. Rest them on a wire rack.

Pipe some of the mash in the centre of a bowl and rest the sausages on top, followed by a spoonful of red onion marmalade and then pour over the sauce. Add the blackened onion petals and dress with a little onion oil and serve.

THE ULTIMATE BEEF BURGER

Makes 8 burgers

600g beef short rib, minced

325g beef chuck, minced

325g beef brisket, minced

Table salt

Brioche buns

1kg Paris brown cup mushrooms, finely diced

200g unsalted butter

200g banana shallots, finely diced

2 cloves of garlic, finely diced

25ml chardonnay vinegar

330ml brown chicken stock (see page 153)

120g mushroom reduction (see recipe for beef tartar on page 102)

2 tbsp runny honey

1 large gherkin, thinly sliced

1kg sweet white onions, thinly sliced

Mayonnaise (see page 148)

Emmenthal cheese slices

1 beefsteak tomato, thinly sliced

Vegetable oil

Combine all of the minced beef and carefully and add 1% of table salt to the total weight of the mince and gently mix, without squashing the meat together too much as this will make the burger tough.

Weigh the mince in to 150g balls.

Gently mould each ball into a patty then place them on a tray lined with greaseproof paper, cover with cling film and place in the fridge for a minimum of 6 hours.

Heat a large heavy based pan until smoking hot and add a little vegetable oil, then heavily caramelise the sliced white onions in small batches until they are brown all over and begin to crisp. When they are all caramelised place them in a bowl and stir in 10g of table salt, remove the pan from the heat, cover them and let them steam themselves for 30 minutes and set aside until needed.

Heat a large heavy based pan and melt the butter, add the mushrooms and cook them over a medium heat until they are browned all over and any liquid that has come out of them has evaporated. Stir in the shallots and garlic and cook them out with the mushrooms for 10 minutes, then add the stock and cook until it has reduced by two thirds. Stir in the mushroom reduction and simmer until the liquid thickens. Add the vinegar and cook for 5 minutes then add the honey and remove from the heat.

Season the mushrooms with table salt to taste if needed and set aside until needed.

Place the mushrooms and onions into two separate pans and put them on a gentle heat to warm through.

Heat a frying pan until smoking and add a little vegetable oil, fry the burgers on each side for 20 seconds until each side is heavily browned and the core temperature of the burger reaches 50°c, then place a spoonful of the mushrooms followed by a slice of cheese on each burger and place the pan under the grill briefly to melt the cheese.

Remove the pan from the grill and place it back on the heat. Place the brioche buns in the pan with the burgers and add a splash of water to the hot pan, then immediately cover the pan with a stainless steel bowl and remove the pan from the heat. Leave the burgers and buns to steam for 1 minute.

Remove the bowl, the core temperature of the burgers should now have reached 56°c. Rest the burgers whilst building the buns.

Place a small spoonful of mayonnaise on the bottom of the bun, then a generous spoonful of the onions, the burger, then more mushrooms, slices of gherkin and tomato, followed by the top of the bun and serve immediately.

PIZZAS

This is how it's done properly. Authentic doppio zero flour from Naples makes up the base of our pizzas, and the toppings come in the form of braised meats, spicy Nduja sausage and fresh vegetables grown locally. We've also got less traditional options like the salmon, goats' cheese and lemon pizza, which is a fresh, light and fragrant alternative to cheesy tomato-based recipes. If you're after something completely different, sweeten things up with our marshmallow and Nutella dessert pizza.

HOW TO COOK PIZZA AT HOME

Begin by heating the grill on its highest setting, meanwhile heat a heavy cast iron pan with a long handle over a high heat for at least 20 minutes, then turn it upside down and slide it under the grill so the base of the pan is as close to the grill as it can be, but make sure you leave about two inches for the pizza to fit between them.

(Alternatively if you are fortunate enough to have a pizza oven, then you will know what to do!)

Lightly flour the work surface using the pizza flour.

Place the dough ball on to the floured work surface and gently flatten it, working from the centre of the dough, pushing your fingers in a down and outwards clockwise motion gently. Keep pushing the dough until you have reached a desired shape and size and you have a nice crust around the pizza base.

Once you have your pizza base, carefully lift it onto the pizza peel or baking sheet. Using a ladle, place the pizza sauce in one pile into the centre of the pizza base and then using the back of the ladle work your way outwards in a circular motion until the sauce is evenly spread across the dough. Make sure you leave 1-2cm around the edge for the crust.

Arrange the toppings as per recipe.

Carefully slide the pizza onto the base of the cast iron pan and immediately slide the pan back under the grill as quickly as possible so you don't lose any heat.

Leave the pizza for around 90 seconds or until the dough begins to bubble around the rim and brown up, and the topping begins to caramelise slightly.

MARGHERITA

1 dough ball (see page 157)

80g pizza sauce (see page 157)

1 clove of garlic, finely sliced

60g cows' milk mozzarella

Extra virgin olive oil

Sea salt

Fresh basil leaves

Follow the instructions in the basic recipes section on how to prepare the dough ball and the sauce. For how to cook the pizza, see page 75.

Starting from the middle of the pizza base, ladle the pizza sauce on top and spread it across the base leaving a little gap around the edges for a nice crust.

Sprinkle the sliced garlic on top of the sauce and then the mozzarella, then the fresh basil and cook.

Season the pizza with olive oil and sea salt before serving.

PIGGIE SMALLS

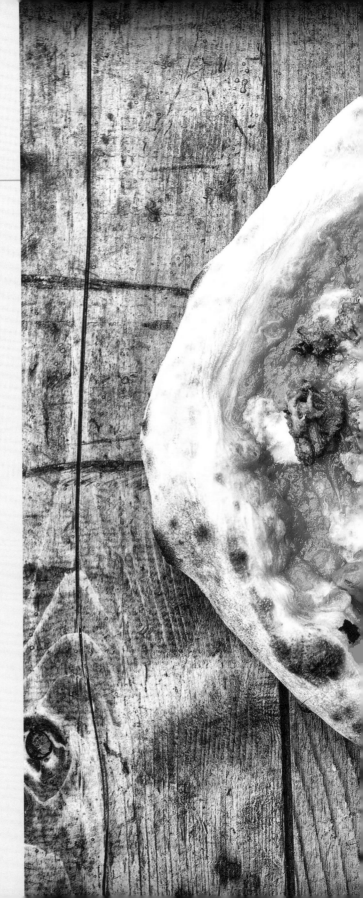

1 dough ball (see page 157)

80g pizza sauce (see page 157)

125g pulled pork shoulder
(see page 146)

Frazzles (crisps), broken up

25g smoked bacon, sliced

60g fior di latte mozzarella

Sea salt

Extra virgin olive oil

Follow the instructions in the basic recipes section on how to prepare the dough ball and the sauce. For how to cook the pizza, see page 75.

Gently scatter the mozzarella over the sauce, then the pulled pork and finally the smoked bacon. Sprinkle with a little sea salt and a healthy drizzle of extra virgin olive oil.

Remove from the oven, scatter with the frazzles and serve.

CRAFTY CUTS

1 dough ball (see page 157)

80g pizza sauce (see page 157)

80g pulled ox cheek (we use the same recipe as we do for our pulled pork on page 146 but reduce the cooking time by around two hours)

6 slices salsiccia piccante a fette peperoni

60g fior di latte mozzarella

50g red onion marmalade (see page 156)

Sea salt

Extra virgin olive oil

Basil leaves

Follow the instructions in the basic recipes section on how to prepare the dough ball and the sauce. For how to cook the pizza, see page 75.

Gently scatter the mozzarella over the sauce, then the pulled ox cheek, red onion jam and finally the piccante a fette. Sprinkle with a little sea salt and a healthy drizzle of extra virgin olive oil then cook.

Sprinkle with the basil leaves and serve.

MARINARA

1 dough ball (see page 157)

80g pizza sauce (see page 157)

5 smoked anchovies

A few Puglia olives

1 clove of garlic

Basil leaves

Sea salt

Extra virgin olive oil

Follow the instructions in the basic recipes section on how to prepare the dough ball and the sauce. For how to cook the pizza, see page 75.

Slice the garlic clove as thin as you possibly can using a mandoline Arrange the anchovies, sliced garlic and olives over the pizza sauce. Lay some basil leaves over it then sprinkle with sea salt and drizzle some olive oil generously on it, cook and serve.

CHOCOLATE & MARSHMALLOW BREAD WITH PECAN PRALINE

1 dough ball (see page 157)

Nutella

Marshmallows

50g caster sugar

25g pecan nuts

Vanilla ice cream to serve

Anise hyssop flowers

75g ricotta

Place the sugar and nuts in a heavy based pan and cook over a low heat until the sugar caramelises and the nuts are toasted. Pour onto a baking sheet lined with greaseproof paper and leave to cool. Then place in a food processor and pulse to a course crumb-like consistency. Store in an airtight container until needed.

Follow the instructions in the basic recipes section on how to prepare the dough ball. For how to cook the pizza, see page 75.

In replacement of the pizza sauce, spread the ricotta evenly over the pizza base using the back of a spoon starting from the middle and working your way out until the whole base is covered, apart from a small 1.5cm rim around the edges. Spoon over some Nutella.

Generously scatter the marshmallows over the top.

Once cooked, sprinkle the praline and the anise hyssop over the top of the sweet pizza and serve with vanilla ice cream.

NDUJA

1 dough ball (see page 157)

80g pizza sauce (see page 157)

60g cows milk mozzarella

Fresh basil leaves

5 tsp nduja (spicy Calabrian sausage meat)

Sea salt

1 clove garlic, finely sliced

Follow the instructions in the basic recipes section on how to prepare the dough ball and the sauce. For how to cook the pizza, see page 75.

Starting from the middle of the pizza base, ladle the pizza sauce on top and spread it across the base leaving a little gap around the edges for a nice crust.

Sprinkle the sliced garlic on top of the sauce and then the mozzarella, nduja and fresh basil.

Season the pizza with a little sea salt before serving.

SMOKED SALMON, RICOTTA, PICKLED LEMON, SORREL, NASTURTIUM & RAMSON CAPERS

1 dough ball (see page 157)

75g ricotta cheese

Slices of pickled lemon (see page 149)

110g oak smoked salmon

Fresh sorrel leaves

Nasturtium leaves

Hedgerow capers (see page 152)

Sea salt

Lemon infused extra virgin olive oil

Follow the instructions in the basic recipes section on how to prepare the dough ball. For how to cook the pizza, see page 75.

On this pizza we use a ricotta cheese in replacement of our pizza sauce as the creaminess and acidity works so well with the smoked salmon.

Place the ricotta in the centre of the base as you would if you were using the pizza sauce, use the back of a spoon to spread the ricotta in an outwards direction to the rim and repeat this process all over the base until it is evenly covered.

Now scatter the smoked salmon over the ricotta, then some pickled lemon slices. Sprinkle with a little sea salt and drizzle the lemon oil all over the pizza then cook.

Once cooked, scatter the sorrel, nasturtium and ramson capers over the top of the pizza and serve.

TANDOORI CHICKEN

1 dough ball (see page 157)

80g pizza sauce (see page 157)

3 cloves of garlic, finely sliced

1 free-range chicken breast

1 tsp tandoori spice rub

125g natural yoghurt

¼ cucumber, peeled and de-seeded, grated

1 tbsp mint leaves, finely sliced

1 small green chilli (seeds removed), finely diced

Sea salt

Fresh coriander leaves

Pinch toasted cumin seeds

100g vegetable oil

Bombay mix

Table salt

Freshly ground black pepper

Follow the instructions in the basic recipes section on how to prepare the dough ball and the sauce. For how to cook the pizza, see page 75.

Marinate the chicken in the spice mix for 2 hours and leave at room temperature.

Place the chicken breast in the oven at 90°c and cook until the core temperature reaches 62°c then let it cool and cut into slices.

To make the raita, place the grated cucumber in a tea towel and squeeze out all of the juice and then add the cucumber to the yoghurt, chilli and mint and stir together. Season with table salt and black pepper to taste.

Place 50g fresh coriander, the cumin seeds, vegetable oil, garlic and a little sea salt in a pestle mortar and grind to a loose paste.

Starting from the middle of the pizza base, ladle the pizza sauce on top and spread it across the base leaving a little gap around the edges for a nice crust.

Place the sliced chicken on top of the sauce and season with a little sea salt. Once cooked, drizzle over the raita, coriander paste, Bombay mix and fresh coriander, serve immediately.

TRUFFLE SALAMI,
SPROUTING BROCCOLI AND CHILLI

1 dough ball (see page 157)

80g pizza sauce (see page 157)

7 slices truffle salami

Red chillies (seeds removed), thinly sliced

50g buffalo mozzarella

4 sprouting broccoli stems, blanched

Fennel shoots

Extra virgin olive oil

Smoked sea salt

Follow the instructions in the basic recipes section on how to prepare the dough ball and the sauce. For how to cook the pizza, see page 75.

Tear the mozzarella into pieces and place it on top of the pizza sauce, arrange the slices of truffle salami and a little sliced chilli on top then add the broccoli. Season the pizza with smoked sea salt and a little olive oil.

Once it is cooked, dress the pizza with some fennel shoots and serve.

YORKSHIRE GOATS' CHEESE, YOUNG FURNANCE PARK LEEKS, HENDERSON'S RELISH KETCHUP AND PUFFED PUMPKIN SEEDS

1 dough ball (see page 157)

60g pizza sauce (see page 157)

60g goats' cheese

30g red onion marmalade (see page 156)

4 young leeks, cleaned (we grow our own at our kitchen gardens at Furnace Park)

For the Henderson's Relish ketchup

125ml Henderson's Relish

1.35g agar agar (available in good supermarkets and health food shops)

1 tbsp pumpkin seeds

Vegetable oil

Sea salt

Follow the instructions in the basic recipes section on how to prepare the dough ball and the sauce. For how to cook the pizza, see page 75.

For the Henderson's ketchup. Place the Henderson's Relish in to a small saucepan and bring to the boil, then gradually whisk in the agar agar and lower the heat to a simmer. Continuously whisk the liquid for 2 minutes and then immediately pour through a fine sieve over an ice bath (a bowl of water and ice) and leave until it is cold and set.

Place the set gel into a blender and blitz until smooth, then pass through a fine sieve and keep in the fridge.

Heat a little vegetable oil to 220°c, then carefully add the pumpkin seeds, they will begin to puff up. Immediately remove them from the hot oil and place on kitchen paper to drain, season with sea salt and let them cool. Keep in an airtight container.

Arrange the young leeks on top of the pizza sauce, then the red onion marmalade. Lay the goats' cheese over the top and the sprinkle with a little sea salt and cook.

Once cooked, place some dots of the ketchup on top and a sprinkle of the pumpkin seeds and serve.

TREAT
YOURSELF

When cooking at home, few attempt to tackle the kind of food that can be found on menus up and down the country. Pork belly, rump of lamb and pigs' head may be cuts of meat that seem daunting when you're not used to handling them on a daily basis, but a lot of this down to lack of confidence. The following recipes guide you through how to prepare and cook these dishes, along with all of the complementary accompaniments that you're accustomed to in our restaurants. Whether it's a special occasion or you're simply feeling a bit indulgent, give these a go and serve yourself up some restaurant quality food at home.

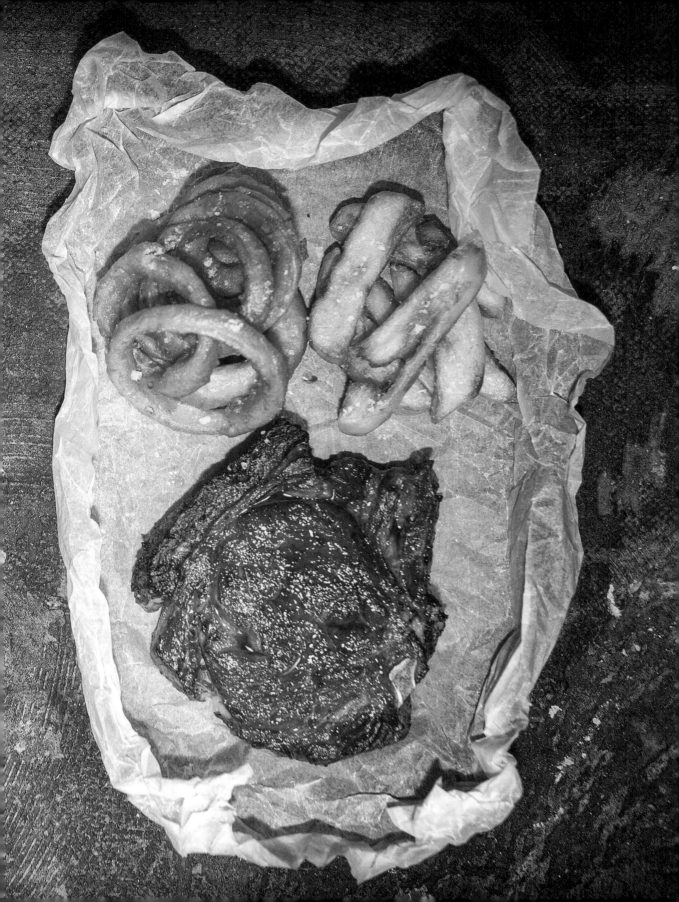

BELLY OF PORK,
PEARL SPELT, BACON & CEPS

Serves 4. This dish takes 4 days to prepare.

½ pork belly, boneless

2 litres of water

430g table salt

100g muscovado sugar

4g pink salt

5g garlic, peeled and crushed

10 sprigs of thyme

50g coriander seeds

1g cloves

2g juniper berries

5g star anise

2g bay leaves

Zest from 1 orange

100g pearl spelt

400g brown chicken stock (see page 153)

Unsalted butter, for the spelt

4 juniper berries

50g chardonnay vinegar

300g Gewurztraminer wine

100g smoked bacon, diced

15g garlic, diced

70g banana shallots, diced

130g sweet white onions, diced

30g chives, finely sliced

10 ceps, trimmed and sliced in half

Mushroom oil (see page 151)

Caster sugar

Table salt

Place the water, 430g table salt, muscovado sugar, pink salt, orange zest, thyme, bay leaves, garlic, coriander seeds, cloves and juniper berries and bring to the boil. Remove from the heat and chill completely then submerge the belly into the brine and place it in the fridge for 48 hours.

After 48 hours, rinse the belly under cold running water for 20 minutes, then pat dry.

Place the belly in a vacuum bag and seal on full pressure and place in a water bath at 65°c and cook for 36 hours.

(Alternatively use the zip-lock bag method on page 14.)

Once cooked, remove the belly and let it cool enough to handle. Place the belly (still in the bag) on to a large flat tray lined with greaseproof paper and then place another piece of greaseproof paper and another tray with a light weight on top of it. Place in the fridge for 12 hours to chill and set.

Once the belly has pressed, remove them from the bag and carefully remove the skin making sure you leave a good layer of fat on it. Then portion into 150g pieces and set aside in the fridge until needed.

Place the portions of belly back into a vacuum bag and reheat in a water bath until it reaches a core temperature of 65°c. (See page 14 for the alternative method.)

Place a heavy based pan on a medium heat and melt 80g of unsalted butter, then add the shallot and onion and cook out until they become translucent and soft, add the garlic, juniper berries and bacon and cook out for 5 minutes, then add the vinegar and cook until it has completely evaporated. Repeat this process with the wine. Add the spelt and chicken stock and cook out over a low heat until the spelt is tender and the liquid has the consistency of a thick sauce.

Remove from the heat and season to taste with table salt if necessary, stir in the chives and set aside until needed.

Remove the portions of belly from the bag and score the fat slightly in a criss-cross pattern, then dust the fat with a little caster sugar and caramelise it using a propane fuelled blow torch, then set aside to rest. If you do not have a blow torch, place under a very hot grill.

Heat a frying pan and cook the ceps quickly in a little mushroom oil until tender and caramelised, season with salt to taste and set aside.

Arrange the dish attractively in a bowl and serve.

CURRIED LAMB FUDGE

220g caster sugar

380ml double cream

18g table salt

25ml chardonnay vinegar

125g rendered lamb fat

85g unsalted butter, cubed

360ml liquid glucose

200g isomalt

20g curry powder

5g freeze dried tomato powder, optional

Line a shallow baking tray tightly with a double layer of cling film and place in the freezer to chill.

Place the cream, sugar and glucose in a heavy based pan and gently bring to a boil. Increase the heat and cook until it reaches 108°c. Remove the pan from the heat and gradually whisk in the butter and fat, followed by the vinegar and salt.

Pour the fudge into the chilled dessert frame (or shallow container) and place it in the freezer until set. Cut the fudge into cubes and place back in the freezer until needed.

Place the isomalt in a pan and place over a low heat until it has melted, then pour it on to a tray lined with greaseproof paper and leave it to set and cool.

Place the isomalt into a blender with the curry and tomato powder (if using) and blend to a fine powder. Then sieve it over an oven proof tray lined with greaseproof paper.

Place the tray in the oven heated to 160°c until the isomalt has melted back to a liquid state. Immediately remove the tray from the oven and leave it to set at room temperature.

When set, break it into shards, before serving remove the fudge from the freezer and sandwich it between the curry glass, serve immediately.

Tip: Use a sugar thermometer for exact temperatures. See page 145.

TARTAR OF DRY AGED BEEF FLANK, TRUFFLED MARROWBONE, MUSHROOM AND NASTURTIUMS

Serves 4

1kg piece of 52 day dry aged beef flank, sinew removed

2kg shiitake mushrooms, thinly sliced

1.25kg chestnut mushrooms (1kg thinly sliced, leave the rest whole)

1kg button mushrooms, thinly sliced

200g Ruby Port

200g Maderia

100g shimeji mushrooms, whole

4 cloves of garlic, peeled and smashed

50ml ponzu (see page 147)

Sea salt

Table salt

75g unsalted butter

50g black truffle butter (see duck egg and truffle toast page 102)

10g black peppercorns

5 sprigs thyme

2 large marrowbones split

Chardonnay vinegar

20g Tewkesbury mustard

60g shallot, peeled and finely diced

50g pickling liquor (see page 149)

Nasturtium leaves

Onion oil (see page 151)

Pine vinegar (see page 152)

Slices of sourdough

Place a large pressure cooker pan over a high heat and add 20g of vegetable oil and 25g unsalted butter when hot. When the butter is foaming, add the shiitake mushrooms and cook over the highest possible heat, stirring constantly. When the mushrooms are heavily caramelised remove them from the pan and set aside. Repeat this process with 1kg of the sliced chestnut mushrooms and the button mushrooms.

Place all of the caramelised mushrooms back to the pan over a high heat and deglaze with the port and madeira, reduce until it has disappeared.

Add 3kg of cold water to the pan along with the thyme, garlic and peppercorns, bring to a simmer and skim off any residue that appears on the surface then place the lid on and bring to full pressure over a high heat, when at full pressure turn the heat down to low and cook for 1.5 hours.

Remove the pan from the heat and let it cool, then remove the lid and carefully pass the liquid through a fine sieve into a clean pan. Place the pan of stock on a high heat and reduce the liquid rapidly until it is 250g in weight then pass through a fine sieve lined with cheese cloth and cool over an ice bath.

In a large container add 1kg of cold water and whisk in 100g of table salt until it dissolves, then place the marrowbones in it and place in the fridge for 2 hours, repeat this process 5 more times.

Remove the bones from the fridge and drain, then place under cold running water for 30 minutes.

Place the bones, cut side up, in an oven tray and roast them at 180°c until golden. Remove them from the oven then using a thick cloth hold the hot bone and spoon the marrow out from the centre of the bone in to a blender jug. Blitz the marrowbone until it liquidises then pass it through a fine sieve and place it in an electric mixer bowl.

Add the diced shallot, mustard and truffle butter to the marrowbone and then using the whisk attachment on the lowest setting begin to mix the ingredients together. When the marrowbone begins to solidify increase the speed of the mixer to high and leave it until the mixture has aerated and tripled in volume.

Season to taste with table salt and chardonnay vinegar then set aside in a container in the fridge.

Take the mushroom reduction and gently stir in the ponzu then set aside in the fridge.

Trim the shimeji mushrooms to remove the stems then place in a vacuum bag with the pickling liquor and seal at full pressure and leave for 30 minutes. (Alternatively submerge the mushrooms in the liquor and refrigerate for 12 hours.)

Remove the beef from the fridge 2 hours in advance of plating the dish. Trim the outside of the beef to remove any flesh that is hard, dry and discoloured.

Cut the sourdough into small cubes and gently fry in a little of the marrowbone until slightly crispy and set aside until needed.

Using an extremely sharp knife scrape the meat toward you with the blade and then dress with a little of the mushroom reduction.

Whisk together some of the onion oil, pine vinegar and mushroom reduction to taste and set aside.

Slice the remaining 250g of chestnut mushrooms thinly using a mandoline to achieve a cross-section cut of the mushroom and set aside.

Arrange the preparations in a bowl and serve immediately.

PIG'S HEAD, MISO, PICKLED KOHLRABI AND APPLE

Serves 8

1 large pig head

200g caster sugar

5 star anise

100ml ponzu (see page 147)

Small bunch of thyme

5 litres Granny Smith apple juice

2 Granny Smith apples, peeled and cut into 5mm cubes

1 large kohlrabi, peeled

50ml pickling liquor (see page 149)

Miso caramel (see page 152)

200g pork rind, fatless

50g salted butter

Freeze dried apple powder, optional

Apple marigold leaves

Place the sugar in a large pan and heat it gently until a golden caramel is achieved. Add the apple juice, thyme and star anise and bring the liquid to the boil. Remove from the heat and cool completely.

Shave the pig head of any facial hair and then wash it thoroughly, especially inside the ears. Place the pig head in a large deep pressure cooker and then pour over the apple caramel liquid. Place the lid on and bring the pan gently up to full pressure over a high heat.

Reduce the heat to a low setting and continue to cook for 2.5 hours. Remove the pan from the heat and reduce the pressure, then remove the lid and allow the liquid and the pig head to cool so you can handle it.

Remove the pig head carefully from the pan and rest it on a tray. Pass the liquid through a fine sieve and skim any residue and fat that floats on the surface. Return the liquid to a clean pan and reduce over a low heat until it is reduced to 300g in weight. Pass the liquid through a fine sieve and then stir in the ponzu and set aside.

Carefully remove the skin from the face of the pig and discard. Pull away all of the flesh from the skull and place it in a bowl, making sure you get right behind the bones. Pick through the meat carefully to remove any cartilage and excess fat.

Add the reduced cooking liquid to the pig head meat gradually, mixing it together but being careful not to break the meat down too much. It should be moist but not wet so if you have any liquid left over then freeze it for the next time you make a terrine. Check the seasoning as the ponzu should do most of this for you, also bearing in mind the miso is very strong and salty too, so season the meat carefully with a little salt if necessary.

Line a shallow tray with a double layer of cling film and make sure there are no creases. Then carefully place the meat inside it and fold the cling film over the top. Place a duplicate tray of the same size over the top and then place a light weight on top to press it. Place it on a level surface inside the fridge and leave it for at least 12 hours to set.

Place the butter in a small pan and heat it until it is foaming and turns brown, remove from the heat and pass through a fine sieve into a jug.

Place the pork rind into a vacuum bag and pour in the brown butter and seal it at full pressure, then place it in a waterbath at 88°c for 12 hours. (Alternatively use the method on page 14.)

Remove it from the bag and pat dry, then place it on a tray in an oven set to 60°c and dehydrate the skin until it has a brittle texture and has shrunk in size. Remove and let it cool on kitchen paper, then store in an airtight container at room temperature.

Cut the kohlrabi into spaghetti or very think match sticks and place in a vacuum bag with the pickling liquor, seal at full pressure and keep in the fridge (alternatively place the Kohlrabi and pickling liquor in a container and refrigerate for 12 hours.)

Place the apple cubes in a vacuum bag on their own and seal at full pressure, repeat this process 8 times and then keep in the fridge. Remove the terrine from the fridge and carefully cut it into 10x2x2cm lengths and set aside.

Heat the oil in a deep fryer (or a deep pan if you don't have one) to 180°c, break the pork rind into shards and deep fry in small batches until it has puffed up and is crispy. Remove from the oil and season with table salt.

Lay a few drops of miso caramel in a bowl and place the piece of terrine on top, then a little more miso caramel on top. Arrange the pickled kohlrabi and Granny Smith apple over and around it, then lay some pieces of pork rind around and season the whole dish with freeze dried apple powder and some of the apple marigold.

BEEF TONGUE & CHEEK, CELERIAC PURÉE AND GREENS

Serves 4. This dish takes 4 days to prepare.

2 beef cheeks, sinew removed

200ml meat glaze (see page 148)

25ml vegetable stock (see page 155)

50ml vegetable oil

1 beef tongue

145g table salt

9g pink salt

200g celeriac, peeled and finely sliced

100ml whole milk

150ml double cream

5g fresh horseradish, finely grated

White truffle oil

Preheat a waterbath to 62°c.

Place each beef cheek, 25ml of vegetable oil and 75ml of meat glaze in two separate vacuum bags and seal on full pressure then place in the waterbath and cook for 72 hours.

(Alternatively use the method on page 14, however you will have to keep a close eye on the water level as it will evaporate rather a lot over this period of time.)

The day before the beef cheeks are due to finish cooking, place 1 litre of cold water in a pan with the salts and whisk well to dissolve them in to the water. Place the beef tongue in the liquid and make sure the pan is tall enough so it is covered completely. Wrap the pan tightly with a double layer of cling film and tin foil then place the pan in the oven heated to 90°c for 11 hours.

Place the celeriac, milk and cream in a heavy based saucepan and gently heat to a simmer, cook until the liquid has reduced and the celeriac is soft and falling apart. Place the contents of the pan into a blender and blitz to a smooth purée. Season with table salt and a little truffle oil to taste then pass the purée through a fine sieve and keep in the fridge.

When the beef cheeks are done, remove them from the waterbath and let them rest in the bags at room temperature for 15 minutes, then open the bags and drain the liquid off and set it to one side. Slice the beef cheeks in half, pour the remaining liquid back over them and rest them in the fridge.

Remove the tongue pan from the oven and let it cool slightly, then plunge the pan into an ice bath (a bowl of water and ice) to chill the tongues completely. Once chilled, remove the tongue from the liquid and peel away the skin from around the tongue and discard it. Cut it into cubes and set aside in the fridge. Discard the cooking liquid.

Place the beef cheek slices onto a tray and put in an oven at 90°c, heat the celeriac purée gently in a pan, then place the cubes of tongue and the remaining 50ml of meat glaze and vegetable stock in a pan and warm it through. Add the fresh horseradish, remove it from the heat and cover with a lid. Leave the sauce to infuse whilst the beef cheeks reach a core temperature of 60°c.

Place a spoonful of the purée on a plate, place the beef cheek beside it and spoon over the tongue and horseradish sauce.

Serve with steamed seasonal greens.

PORTERHOUSE STEAK, CHIPS AND ONION RINGS

Serves 2 to share. The steak needs to cure for 2 days.

1 Porterhouse steak, weighing approximately 1kg

Chips (see page 66)

Beer batter (see page 156)

2 sweet white onions

Table salt

Black pepper

Grapeseed oil

Vegetable oil

Sea salt

Place the steak on a wire cooling rack set over a tray and place in the fridge uncovered for 2 days.

Remove the steak from the fridge and leave it to come to room temperature before cooking.

Prepare the chips to the point where they are ready for the final fry.

Peel the onions whole and slice into 1cm thick rings, then sprinkle a little table salt over them and leave them to absorb the salt for 5 minutes. Then rinse them under cold running water to wash away the salt and pat dry on kitchen paper. Set aside until needed.

Heat a heavy based frying pan large enough to fit the steak in until smoking, then add some grapeseed oil to the pan.

Season the steak on both sides with table salt and carefully place it in the hot oil, make sure you move the steak around the pan to get an even browning and carefully turn the steak over every 20 seconds. Continue to do this for 5-6 minutes then remove it from the pan and let the steak rest on a wire rack set over a tray for 10 minutes.

Whilst the steak is resting, finish frying the chips and then set aside on kitchen paper.

Dip the onion rings into the beer batter and deep fry in vegetable oil heated to 180°c and cook them until golden, turning them occasionally. Let them drain on kitchen paper and season the onion rings and chips with sea salt.

Grind a little black pepper over the steak on both sides and serve with the chips and onion rings.

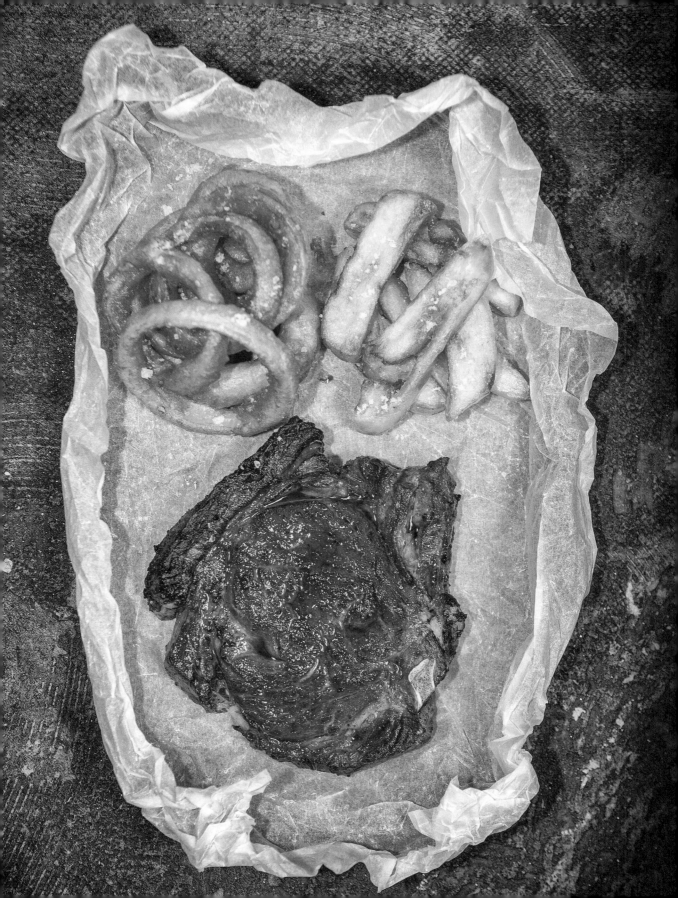

RUMP OF LAMB, FERMENTED ONION AND APPLE CARAMEL, PICKLED CUCUMBER, PEAS, BEANS & HERBS

Serves 4. This dish takes 7 days for onion preparation.

1 kg lamb rump, sinew removed

10 white onions, peeled and thinly sliced

Table salt

2 litres fresh Cox's apple juice

1 cucumber, peeled and cut into 5mm cubes

2kg fresh peas, podded (keep the pods)

250g broad beans, podded

150g crème fraiche

70ml pickling liquor (see page 149)

Grapeseed oil

Onion oil (see page 151)

Jasmine tea

Sea salt

Nasturtium leaves

Chocolate mint leaves

Chocolate mint flowers

Sweet cicely leaves

Flowering leek buds

Place a pan over a high heat and add a little vegetable oil. When hot fry the sliced onions in batches until heavily caramelised and burnt then weigh them. Add 2% of their weight in table salt and then place them in a vacuum bag and seal at full pressure whilst they are hot. Leave at room temperature for 1 hour then transfer them to the fridge and leave them for 7 days.

(Alternatively use the method on page 14.)

Place the lamb rump on kitchen paper and pat it dry, then place on a wire cooling rack set above a tray and leave it uncovered in the fridge for 1 day.

Place the apple juice in a pan and very slowly reduce it until it has caramelised and becomes a thick sweet and sour syrup weighing approximately 200g. Cool and keep in the fridge.

After 7 days remove the onions from the fridge and pass them through a juicer and then a fine sieve into a new container. Weigh out 100g of the thick onion juice and then gently whisk in 50g of the apple caramel, set aside and keep in the fridge.

Pass the pea pods and half of the podded peas through a juicer and then a fine sieve and set aside in the fridge over an ice bath.

Bring a pan of water to the boil and season it heavily with salt. Blanch the remaining peas and beans in the water for 20 seconds then immediately refresh in iced water. Drain and pat dry with kitchen paper then set aside in the fridge.

Place the cucumber in a vacuum bag with the pickling liquor and seal at full pressure, then open the bag and seal again, repeat this process 8 times. (Alternatively place both the cucumber and liquor into a container and refrigerate for 12 hours.)

Place a frying pan over a low heat. Season the lamb on the fat side only with a generous helping of table salt then place it fat side down in to the dry pan and push down gently for 1 minute until the fat begins to render. Move the lamb around the pan carefully on the skin side for 7 minutes until the fat has rendered and it is caramelised. Season the flesh with a little table salt.

Add 50g of unsalted butter and a pinch of jasmine tea to the pan and gently baste the flesh with it for 2 minutes. Then place the pan in an oven at 175°c for around 12 minutes or until the core temperature of the rump reaches 56°c, making sure to baste the lamb every few minutes.

Remove the lamb and rest it on a wire cooling rack set above a tray and pour the cooking fat back over the skin.

Meanwhile weigh out 100g of the pea juice and place in a small saucepan with 40g onion oil and whisk it together gently, season with table salt to taste. Warm it to 50°c over a very low heat then remove it and set aside. Add some of the pickled cucumber, blanched peas, beans and stir it together. Slice the lamb, arrange the preparations carefully on a deep plate and serve.

THE MILESTONE COOKERY SCHOOL

Led by our expert team, along with a few special guests, we host cookery classes offering hands on training in everything from basic bread courses to butchering, curing and cooking a whole pig in a day.

Using top quality local produce, learn how to make your own black pudding, hone your knife skills, get to grips with pasta and gnocci or find out how to whip up superb street food. Our classes are all about extending our cooking ethos into the wider community. Whilst we want people to visit our restaurants as much as possible, we know it's

obviously not feasible to eat out every day. So we want to encourage people to cook and prepare food like we do. It's all about making use of local producers – go to your butchers, fishmongers and greengrocers for great quality and value food that keeps the food miles down, and the flavour up. And with that utilise every cut, make the most out of the seasons and approach home cooking with a bit of innovation and an open mind. So that's where we come in, aiming to give you the skills to be able to do this.

We provide all of the ingredients, equipment and know-how, guiding you through each stage step by step in an informal, relaxed environment. It doesn't matter if you get it wrong, if your bread's not quite up to scratch or if you burn your first batch of brownies – it's about giving it a go, trying something new and stepping out of your comfort zone.

Whether it's a one off half-day class, a few in a row you'll be sure to leave with a bit of extra knowledge and sense of pride and achievement. And your evening meal, of course.

SWEET
TOOTH

Our desserts have always been the subject of high praise, in fact when we once tried to take our famed sticky toffee pudding off the Milestone menu for a period of time, we actually got complaints. Alas, it wasn't long until we saw the error of our ways, and we have learned not to challenge popular opinion since. Our lighter desserts also go down a treat. When in season one of the best ways to enjoy strawberries is with our goats' milk, white chocolate, apple and sorrel recipe. Another that utilises our crops for something sweeter is the yoghurt sorbet with rhubarb jam and sweet cicely. Rhubarb grows throughout the year and varies in flavour depending on seasons, so this is a great dessert to experiment with all year round.

STICKY TOFFEE PUDDING

Serves 4

300g pitted dates

300ml water

300g unsalted butter, softened

300g soft dark brown sugar

300g self-raising flour, sieved

10g table salt

5g bicarbonate of soda

8 large eggs, beaten

250ml whipping cream

200g muscovado sugar

125g salted butter

50ml black treacle

100g pecan nuts

1 egg white

50g caster sugar

Place the dates and water in a pan and bring to the boil. Remove from the heat and stir in the bicarbonate of soda and then pulse the mixture with a hand blender and set aside.

Place the unsalted butter and soft dark brown sugar in an electric mixing bowl with the paddle attachment and begin to mix them together until the mixture becomes pale and creamy. Add the beaten egg a little at a time to avoid splitting the mixture then gradually add the date mixture until it is fully incorporated.

Add salt to the flour and then add the flour in 3 stages on the lowest speed setting, allowing the mixture to be fully combined before adding the next lot of flour (Alternatively, follow this procedure step-by-step by using a large mixing bowl and a spatula.)

Preheat the oven to 150°c. Lightly grease the moulds you wish to bake the pudding in and then carefully pour in the batter and leave a good half inch gap at the top as the pudding will rise significantly. Place the moulds gently onto a tray and bake in the oven for 30-40 minutes, until dark golden brown and when you pierce a knife into the centre of the pudding it comes out clean and very hot to the touch.

Remove the puddings from the oven and allow them to cool in the moulds before removing and cooling them further on a wire rack.

Place the egg whites in a bowl and whisk them until they become frothy. Carefully dip the pecans in the egg white one by one making sure they are evenly coated and there is no excess egg white on them. Transfer them to a bowl containing the caster sugar and toss them in it to coat them completely.

Preheat an oven to 160°c.

Place a sheet of greaseproof paper on a baking sheet and then place the sugar coated pecans on top making sure they are evenly spaced. Place the tray in the oven and cook them for around 10-15 minutes until they are golden and crisp. Make sure you turn them a few times during cooking so they cook evenly.

Place the muscovado sugar, treacle and salted butter in a heavy based saucepan and gently heat over a low temperature until the butter has melted and the sugar begins to mix into it. Make sure you stir it constantly. When mixed together, increase the heat until it begins to bubble and caramelise, then gradually add the whipping cream whilst whisking the sauce together. Boil the sauce for 2 minutes then remove from the heat and let it cool a little.

To serve, put a little of the sauce in a microwaveable container and place a pudding on top. Put a lid on the container and microwave for 30 seconds and then carefully turn the pudding over so that it absorbs the sauce evenly throughout. Put the lid back on and return it to the microwave for a further 30 seconds.

Warm some sauce up separately, carefully transfer the pudding to a bowl and add a little pool of sauce next to the pudding, add some of the candied pecans and serve with ice cream.

ROBIN OF LOCKSLEY,
CHEWY RHUBARB AND APPLE MARIGOLD

Serves 8

75ml Robin of Locksley gin

225g caster sugar

125ml water

25ml lime juice

3 pasteurised egg whites

100ml grenadine

100ml Champagne

250g skinny Victoria rhubarb, washed and cut into 10cm batons

Apple marigold leaves

Place 125g sugar and the water in a pan and heat to dissolve then cool over an ice bath (a bowl of water and ice) immediately.

Using a handheld blender, blitz the egg whites briefly to break them, then stir in the sugar syrup (sugar and water mixture), lime juice and gin and set aside in the fridge.

Place a cream whipper in the freezer for half an hour to chill completely.

When the whipper is cold, pour the gin mixture into it and charge it with two nitrous oxide bulbs and shake it well for 2 minutes, then keep in the fridge for at least 2 hours until needed.

Combine the grenadine and 100g sugar and heat to dissolve, then chill over an ice bath. Once chilled stir in the Champagne and set aside.

Place the rhubarb into 4 vacuum bags and split the Champagne mixture between them, then seal on full pressure and place in a water bath set to 86°c. Cook until they are tender. When cooked, cool the bags in an ice bath completely.

Open the bags and strain off the liquid and reduce it to a syrup over a low heat. Then whilst the syrup is still hot, dip the rhubarb into it to coat and then place on a tray lined with greaseproof paper. Dehydrate it at 60°c in the oven or a dehydrator until it is shrivelled and reduced in size and it has a chewy texture, then set aside.

Carefully release the gin mousse from the whipper into a bowl, then place some rhubarb next to it with some apple marigold and serve.

STRAWBERRIES, GOATS' MILK, CARAMELISED WHITE CHOCOLATE, APPLE & SORREL

Serves 8

200ml goats' milk

200ml double cream

250g caster sugar

1.5 leaves of gelatine

Table salt

15ml lemon juice

200g fructose

1kg fresh strawberries, for purée

Fresh strawberries, quarted for garnish

150g white chocolate

200g Granny Smith apple juice

150ml sorrel juice

50g icing sugar

Freeze dried strawberries, optional

Fresh sorrel leaves

To make the strawberry purée, blend 1kg of strawberries and 200g caster sugar until smooth. Pass through a fine sieve and set aside until needed.

Place the goats' milk, cream and 50g caster sugar in a pan and gently warm to dissolve the sugar. Bloom (soak) the gelatine in cold water then stir the gelatine into the warm liquid and season with the lemon juice and a little table salt to taste, pass through a fine sieve into a jug. Let the liquid cool slightly then pour it into circular moulds tightly wrapped in cling film so that the liquid does not leak. Set them on a tray in the fridge until needed.

Place 200g of the strawberry purée and 50g icing sugar in a bowl and whisk together, spread the mixture onto a sheet of greaseproof paper thinly and dehydrate it at 60°c until it is leathery in texture. Remove it from the oven and cut it into desired shapes then store it in an airtight container at room temperature until needed.

Combine 200ml water and 200g fructose together and gently bring to the boil, remove from the heat and add to the remaining strawberry purée then pass through a fine sieve set over an ice bath to chill immediately. Churn in an ice cream machine using the manufacturers guidelines.

Place the chocolate into a vacuum bag and seal on full pressure, place the bag in a pan of boiling water and cook it until the chocolate darkens in colour and caramelises. Remove the bag from the water and allow it to cool naturally. Remove the chocolate from the bag and blitz it to a course crumb and store it in the fridge until needed.

(Alternatively use the method on page 14.)

Combine the sorrel and apple juice, pour it into a container and freeze it solid.

Once frozen, scrape at it using a fork to create a granita, and then keep in the freezer until needed.

Arrange the dish attractively in a bowl and serve immediately.

SPICY STRAWBERRY PASTELS

1kg strawberries, for the purée

380g caster sugar

10g pectin

5g tartaric acid

1 tsp red Tabasco sauce

Freeze dried strawberries, optional

2 tbsps granulated sugar

To make the strawberry purée, blend 1kg of strawberries and 200g caster sugar until smooth. Pass through a fine sieve and set aside until needed.

Combine 400g of the purée with 360g of the sugar in a heavy based pan and bring it to the boil over a medium heat.

In a bowl combine the pectin and the remaining 20g of sugar. When the purée has come to the boil, gradually whisk in the pectin mixture.

Line a shallow container tightly with a double layer of cling film and place it in the fridge to chill.

Slowly bring the mixture to 104°c and then immediately remove the pan from the heat and whisk in the tartaric acid and Tabasco sauce.

Pour the mixture into the chilled dessert frame (or shallow container) and leave it to set for at least 4 hours in the fridge.

Cut the pastels into 2cm squares. Roll each square in granulated white sugar to coat and top with freeze dried strawberries before serving.

Tip: Use a sugar thermometer for exact temperatures. See page 145.

YOGHURT SORBET, RHUBARB JAM & GRANOLA

Serves 8

900g natural yoghurt

150g caster sugar

235ml water

2 leaves of gelatine

Granola (see recipe on page 17)

100g fructose

250g Victoria rhubarb, cut into 5cm pieces

85ml rhubarb juice

135ml grenadine

25ml glucose syrup

Table salt

Fresh chamomile, chrysanthemum and sweet cicely leaves

Heat the caster sugar and 150ml of the water in a pan and bring to a boil, remove from the heat and cool slightly. Bloom (soak) the gelatine in cold water and when soft add it to the warm sugar syrup and stir it to dissolve. Pass through a fine sieve into the yoghurt and stir well to combine. Pass through a fine sieve once more and then churn in an ice cream machine according to the manufacturer's guidelines.

To make the jam, place the remaining 85ml of water, rhubarb juice, fructose, glucose syrup and grenadine in a pan and bring to the boil, lower the heat and add the rhubarb. Cook it very slowly over a low heat until the liquid has almost all evaporated and the rhubarb has absorbed it, season with salt to taste and then remove the pan from the heat and let the mixture cool naturally. Set aside in the fridge until needed.

Place some of the jam in the bottom of a bowl and then a spoon of the sorbet on top, sprinkle over the granola and then arrange the fresh herbs over the dish. Serve immediately.

HAPPY HOUR

Our in-house creations make use of the herbs, fruits and plants that we grow on site. It's time to get creative; infuse your favourite gin, add fresh thyme to a Margarita and make use of seasonal ingredients with drinks like our blackberry and cinnamon cocktail. People are just as discerning about what they are drinking as they are about what they cook these days, so why not stock up your home bar and kick things off with a few of our favourites.

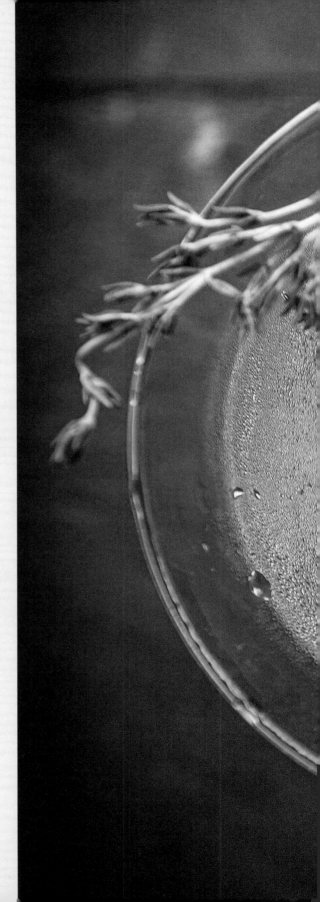

A LIST OF EQUIPMENT

Bar spoon

A long handled spoon used to stir mixed drinks in tall glasses. You can also use the back of the spoon for layering drinks and churning. A bar spoon measure is the equivalent of a teaspoon.

Muddler

Bartenders' tool used for muddling and mashing ingredients in cocktails like a pestle and mortar to release the flavours. Also handy for crushing ice. If you don't have a muddler a rolling pin is the next best thing.

Jigger measure

Set of tools used to measure out ingredients into cocktails. However, at home we prefer to free pour!

Hawthorn strainer

We use this to pour the cocktails out of the Boston tin after shaking or stirring. It stops the ice from escaping. These can be picked up at most supermarkets or online if you want to complete your home cocktail kit.

Boston glass and tin or cocktail shaker

Our preferred shaker is the Boston glass and tin on our bars however both do the same job. A cocktail shaker is a stainless steel two piece tin and lid, sometimes with a built in strainer. The Boston glass and tin is a two piece glass and stainless steel set. We prefer this because it can be used for both shaking and stirring using the glass.

Double strain fine sieve

Most similar to your baking sieve at home, we use smaller versions for our drinks which you can pick up in most baking shops! Use for best results in our gin thyme drink to ensure a crystal clear finish, stopping any broken herbs or fruit from entering after shaking.

HOW TO
AND TIPS

In our methods you should always place your ingredients into the Boston glass when preparing a drink.

How to lock a Boston glass and tin

To lock the glass and tin together before shaking, stirring or rolling simply place the tin wide edge first onto the top of the glass and using the bottom of your palm bang the tin into place firmly. Don't worry the glasses are made of sturdy stuff and shouldn't break.

Use fresh ice in your cocktails

Your drink becomes colder and remains colder for longer. Fresh ice looks better and dilutes slower, givng you a less watered-down flavour.

While water dilution is great for cocktails, going over the top is just too much. You do want water in order to bring out some of the great aromas in your spirits. When you shake your drink the ice in the shaker dilutes just the right amount while bringing down the temperature of your cocktail. If you use that same ice by dumping it into your cocktail you get smaller pieces of ice which melt faster and don't look great!

Tip: Strain your cocktail to hold back the old ice and pour it over a fresh glass with ice. If you're making a martini-style cocktail, strain that chilled beverage into a chilled glass. (One from the freezer is ideal.)

Muddling

To muddle, use a sturdy mixing glass, a pint glass, or a shaker tin.

Place the leaves into the bottom of the glass. Add your sugar, pieces of fruit, or other ingredients that the recipe calls for.

Place the muddler in the glass. Press down with it lightly on the leaves and give a few gentle twists. If there's also fruit in the glass, you should see juice squirting out from the flesh.

When your kitchen smells of the fresh herbs/fruit then you're done!

Churning

Stir the drink with ice using a bar spoon. Top up the glass with more crushed ice and churn again. Repeat this process until the glass is three-quarters full then serve. By churning you are diluting the spirit and infusing the ingredients into the drink.

ENGLISH GARDEN
MOJITO

3 apple wedges

Rosemary sprig

37.5ml Havana Blanco

25ml apple juice

12.5ml sugar syrup

Soda

Place the apple wedge and rosemary into your glass and muddle to squash the apple and rosemary together.

Add 37.5ml Havana blanco, 25ml apple juice, 12.5ml sugar syrup and top with crushed ice and churn together to combine flavours for approximately 1 minute.

Top with crushed ice to the top of the glass and finish with soda water.

Garnish with apple slices and apple marigold or a rosemary sprig.

BLACKBERRY SPICE

50ml Pimm's

10ml elderflower cordial

1 barspoon blackberry compote (see page 154)

6 mint leaves

Splash of lemonade

Pinch cinnamon

Cinnamon stick, to garnish

Sprig of mint, to garnish

2 blackberries, to garnish

Add all the ingredients (except the lemonade and garnishes) to a Collins glass, churn over crushed ice. Top with a splash of lemonade and garnish with a large sprig of mint, blackberries and a cinnamon stick.

NON-ALCOHOLIC
FOREST FRUIT FLING

25ml apple juice

25ml cranberry juice

12.5ml lemon juice

25ml mixed berries

Soda water

Berry compote (See page 154)

Place all ingredients except the berries and soda water into Boston glass and shake with ice. Half fill a Collins glass with crushed ice and pour over the ingredients using a strainer. Top with soda and garnish with a bar spoonful of berries and two sip straws.

ESPRESSO
MARTINI

25ml espresso coffee

25ml Kahlua (coffee liquor)

50ml vodka

12.5ml vanilla sugar syrup

Coffee beans, for garnish

Vanilla pod, optional

Combine all ingredients in a shaker with ice and shake very vigorously to combine. This ensures you get a thick creamy top on your drink.

For best results use ground coffee for your espresso.

Strain into a chilled martini cocktail glass and garnish with four coffee beans placed next to each other on top.

If you don't like the sweetness of the vanilla sugar syrup, try it without.

To keep the vanilla flavour, infuse the vodka instead of sugar syrup by placing an open vanilla pod into the vodka and leave to infuse for at least 7 days.

HEDGEROW ROSEMARY FIZZ

25ml Beefeater gin

25ml sloe gin

25ml apple juice

12.5ml lemon juice

25ml mixed berries

Sprig rosemary

Splash Prosecco

Combine all ingredients except the Prosecco, rosemary and berries into a shaker and shake over ice. Half fill a Collins glass with crushed ice and pour over ingredients. Top with Prosecco and garnish with a bar spoon full of berries, 2 sip straws and rosemary sprig.

Serve in a rocks glass.

GIN
THYME

50ml Beefeater gin

15ml brine from green olives

25ml lemon juice

Dash sugar syrup

Dash orange bitters

2 sprigs thyme

Shake all ingredients gently with ice, then double strain using a hawthorn strainer and fine sieve into a chilled martini glass. Garnish with a sprig of thyme over the glass.

STARTING
FROM SCRATCH

Where possible we aim to make all of our own bread, pizza bases, oils, sauces and stocks. When everything is done from scratch you're able to control exactly what goes into your food, meaning the result will be high quality and maximum flavour. Whether it's a barbecue meat rub, fresh mayonnaise, infused oils, vegetable stock or a simple bread recipe you're after, the next few pages are your go-to guide for basics.

USEFUL KITCHEN EQUIPMENT

Thermomix: A high-powered blender that has the capability to heat and cook whilst blending or stirring foods.

Water bath: Typically a container filled with water and heated to precise temperatures using a heating element. It is used for cooking foods sous vide, which is French for "under vacuum".

Sous vide is a method of cooking in which food is sealed in airtight plastic pouches. It is then placed in a water bath or in a temperature-controlled water environment for longer than normal cooking times, at an accurately regulated temperature much lower than is normally used for cooking. The intent is to cook the food evenly, ensuring that the inside is properly cooked without overcooking the outside, and to retain maximum amount of moisture.

Vacuum packing machine: A machine used to remove air from the inside of a plastic pouch containing foods.

A great tool for maximising shelf life and an essential tool for cooking foods sous vide. It ensures the food is not in direct contact with the water, avoiding all flavour loss and maximising moisture as none can escape from the bag the food is cooked in.

Also used for increasing flavours and reducing marinating times, changing textures of fruits and vegetables, changing viscosities of liquids and so on.

Mandoline: A cutting tool used to slice fruits and vegetables into perfectly consistent slices with a variable width.

Cream whipper: A cream whipper uses nitrous oxide gas charges (N2o) to make cream or such like liquids whipped or aerated. The pressure of the gas inside the whipper forces the liquid out through a whipping device that makes it light and fluffy.

Sugar thermometer: This a cooking thermometer used to precisely measure the temperature of a cooking solution, particularly useful for high temperature liquids such as sugars or fats.

Similar to a regular thermometer however it is able to read temperatures in excess of 200°c.

Ice Cream Machine: An ice cream machine is able to simultaneously freeze the mixture while churning it so as to aerate the mixture and avoid the buildup of ice crystals. It therefore makes the end product far smoother than applying a manual churning technique.

BARBECUE PULLED PORK SHOULDER

2.5kg bone-in pork shoulder, skinless and fatless

750g barbecue dry rub (see page 147)

125g meat glaze (see page148)

Table salt

Cooking time: 1 day.

Massage the dry rub into the pork shoulder and leave it to rest for 12 hours at room temperature in a deep container.

Set up your barbecue (we use a ceramic dome shaped barbecue, perfect for low, slow cooking and smoking – see specialist equipment.)

Make sure you use a mixture of oak wood logs and charcoal, heat the barbecue to 110°c and maintain that temperature.

Place the pork directly on to the grill mesh of the barbecue and close the dome or lid and leave it for 8-12 hours.

After the suggested time period of cooking, the core temperature of the pork shoulder should be 88°c (2 or 3 degrees either side will not matter all too much.) When this temperature is achieved carefully remove the pork from the barbecue and place it in to a large tray and cover it with tin foil. Leave it to rest for at least one hour.

Wearing food safe gloves, begin to slide the meat away from the bones and work it between your fingers into large strands and chunks into a clean bowl or tray.

Add the meat glaze and work it into the pork, and then season to taste if necessary with the table salt and a little more dry rub if you want a spicier kick.

BARBECUE DRY RUB

5g cumin seeds

5g black peppercorns

5g coriander seeds

10g fennel seeds

100g muscovado sugar

50g granulated sugar

10g garlic powder

100g table salt

5g cayenne pepper

30g paprika

5g dried oregano

15g smoked paprika

Toast all of the seeds in a dry pan over a low heat for five minutes until they release their aromas. Remove them from the pan and leave the spices to cool.

Combine with the rest of the ingredients and blitz to a fine powder using a food processor. Keep in an airtight container.

PONZU

80g spring onions, finely chopped

175ml rice wine vinegar

50g golden caster sugar

75g borage honey

30g root ginger, peeled and finely grated

350g 18 month barrel-aged light soy sauce

Combine all of the ingredients together and store in a sterilised Kilner jar in the fridge, it needs to mature for 8 weeks before using. When it is mature and ready to use, pass it through a fine sieve. Store at room temperature.

(To sterilise the jars, wash them thoroughly using hot soapy water and rinse well then place in a preheated oven at 140°c for 20 minutes, remove from the oven and let them cool completely before using.)

MAYONNAISE

50g duck egg yolks	
20g Tewkesbury mustard	
5g table salt	
15ml Chardonnay vinegar	
420ml vegetable oil	

Place all of the ingredients except the oil into a tall jug. Using a stick blender, blend the ingredients together. Gradually pour in the oil a little at a time and blend until all of the oil is emulsified into the mixture.

MEAT GLAZE

2 litres brown chicken stock (see page 153)
125g smoked pork fat
500g dry aged beef rib trimmings
250g banana shallots, finely sliced
75g unsalted butter
250ml Madeira
30ml cider vinegar
200g Heinz tomato ketchup
60g French's American mustard
60ml Henderson's Relish
5ml red Tabasco sauce
100ml fresh russet apple juice
75g molasses
5g Chinese five-spice
Vegetable oil

Heat a a little oil in a large pan, when hot add the beef trim in small batches and heavily caramelise. Place all of the caramelised trim back to the pan and then add the brown chicken stock. Reduce the heat and simmer gently until the liquid has reduced by two thirds, making sure you skim any residue that appears on the surface of the stock. Once the liquid has reduced, set it aside whilst you make the rest of the sauce.

In a new pan add the butter and heat it until foaming, add the shallots and cook them over a low heat until soft and heavily caramelised. Add the Chinese five-spice and cook it out for two minutes then deglaze the pan with the vinegar until it has disappeared. Add the Madeira and reduce the liquid by half.

Add this liquid to the pan of dry aged beef and brown chicken stock, bring it back up to a simmer and reduce gently by half again making sure you are constantly skimming the residue that appears on the surface.

Combine all of the other ingredients (except the pork fat) together in a bowl and then stir in to the stock. Cook the sauce out for five minutes and then pass it through a fine sieve into a container and then finally whisk in the smoked pork fat to emulsify it in to the sauce. Keep it in the fridge until needed.

BERRY VINEGAR

1 litre chardonnay vinegar
1.25kg berries (e.g. blackberries, mulberries, sloes, strawberries, black gooseberries)
125ml water
275g caster sugar

This vinegar takes 2 months to make.

Place the water and 100g of caster sugar in a pan and heat gently until dissolved, then add the berries and simmer for 5 minutes.

Add the vinegar and bring the mixture to the boil and immediately remove from the heat, chill quickly over an ice bath (a bowl of ice and water.) Leave the mixture for 20 days in the fridge covered with cheese cloth. Pass it through a fine sieve and add 175g of caster sugar to the mixture and bring to the boil one more time. Chill then store in a Kilner jar in the fridge for a minimum of 4 weeks to mature before using.

PICKLING LIQUOR

1kg chardonnay vinegar
750g caster sugar
250ml water

Place all of the ingredients in a pan and bring to the boil, then chill. Keep in the fridge.

PICKLED LEMONS

10 lemons, thinly sliced and seeds removed
400ml pickling liquor (see above)

Place the ingredients into a sterilised Kilner jar and leave in the fridge. After 48 hours they are ready to use.

TREACLE AND STOUT BREAD ROLLS

600g T55 white bread flour

250g granary bread flour

100g pumpkin seeds

100g sunflower seeds

100g rolled porridge oats, sieved

60g unsalted butter, softened

75g black treacle, warmed

500ml stout, warmed to 38°c

200ml water, warmed to 38°c

40g fresh yeast

40g table salt

20g marmite, warmed

40g muscovado sugar

Place all of the ingredients except the stout, water and yeast in a large electric mixing bowl using the dough hook attachment. On the lowest setting begin mixing the ingredients. Meanwhile, whisk the yeast in to the warm water, when dissolved cover with cling film and leave for 5 minutes until frothy. Add the yeast mixture to the dry mix gradually until fully incorporated, then add the stout gradually.

Mix on the lowest setting for 5 minutes until a sticky dough is formed, turn off the mixer and let it rest for 5 minutes.

Turn the mixer back on and mix for a further 10 minutes, increase the speed to the next setting and mix for a further 5 minutes. Remove the dough from the mixer and gently roll it into a ball.

Line a large bowl with a little grease spray and place the dough inside and cover tightly with cling film then leave to prove in a warm place for around 1.5 hours.

When the mixture has proved and is triple its size, remove from the bowl onto a lightly greased surface and knock it back, then separate the dough into 40g pieces.

Using the palm of your hand roll the dough into small balls, then place on a heavy baking sheet lightly dusted with flour and cover with a moist tea cloth, leave in a warm place for around 45 minutes until risen.

Remove the cloth and very carefully place in an oven preheated to 220°c for 6 minutes, then reduce the heat to 180°c and continue to cook for around 15 minutes or until the bread is beautiful and golden and if you tap the bottom they sound hollow.

Place on a wire cooling rack, cool and serve immediately.

ONION
OIL

150g green spring onion tops
50g green leek tops
100g chives
15g table salt
600ml vegetable oil

Place all of the ingredients into a Thermomix and blend on speed 8 for 8 minutes at 80°c. Pass through a fine sieve and cool over an ice bath (a bowl of water and ice) immediately. Once chilled, keep in the fridge in a dark place.

(At the restaurant we use a Thermomix, which blends and cooks at the same time, alternatively you could use a high powered blender and blend until the mixture reaches 80°c. This method can be replicated where the use of a Thermomix is used in most recipes.)

BLACKCURRANT
LEAF OIL

300g blackcurrant leaves
600ml vegetable oil
10g table salt

Place all of the ingredients into a Thermomix and blend on speed 8 for 8 minutes at 80°c. Pass through a fine sieve and cool over an ice bath immediately. Once chilled, keep in the fridge in a dark place.

(Alternatively use the method explained above.)

MUSHROOM
OIL

150g dried ceps, ground to a powder
400ml vegetable oil

Takes 2 weeks.

Place all the ingredients into a vacuum bag and seal on full pressure. Cook in a waterbath at 85°c for 12 hours. Remove from the bath and allow to cool naturally. Chill for 2 weeks then pass through a cheesecloth. Store in an airtight container in a cool dark place until needed.

If you do not have a vacuum packing machine or waterbath, you can place the ingredients into a zip-lock style bag and bring a pan of water to 85°c. Immerse the bag into the water, so long as you maintain the correct temperature you will gain the same result.

HEDGEROW CAPERS

Unripe berries or seeds (e.g. unripe elderberries/ramson seeds/unripe blackcurrants/green nasturtium seeds)

10% the berry or seeds' weight in table salt

Pickling liquor (see page 149)

Takes 5 months.

Place the ingredients into a vacuum bag and vacuum on full pressure (alternatively use a Kilner jar, however the curing process will take considerably longer), leave for one month then remove from the bag and place in a sterilised Kilner jar. Pour over just enough pickling liquor to cover and leave in a cool dark place for a minimum of 4 months.

MISO CARAMEL

100g golden caster sugar

70g red miso paste

50ml 18 month barrel-aged light soy sauce

25ml fresh yuzu juice

40ml lime juice

Place the sugar in a heavy based pan and heat until a deep golden caramel is formed, remove from the heat and cool slightly then stir in the miso paste, then the soy sauce, yuzu and lime juice. Transfer the mixture to a clean pan and heat gently. Simmer for 5 minutes. Pour into a blender and blitz until completely smooth, pass through a fine sieve and keep at room temperature.

PINE VINEGAR

100g Douglas Fir pine needles

500g Chardonnay vinegar

50g caster sugar

Place the ingredients into a high powered blender and blend on a high speed until the needles have completely broken down and the vinegar becomes dark green. Place in a vacuum bag and seal on full pressure then leave to infuse for 24 hours at room temperature. Pass through a fine sieve, keep in the fridge in a dark place until needed.

BROWN CHICKEN STOCK

3kg chicken wings

30g milk powder

200g white onion, peeled and finely sliced

200g carrot, peeled and finely sliced

400g chestnut mushrooms, finely sliced

Cold water

10g black peppercorns

5 sprigs of thyme

4 garlic cloves, thinly sliced

Vegetable oil

Place the chicken wings in a large oven tray and sprinkle over the milk powder and roast them in the oven at 175°c until heavily caramelised, making sure to turn them regularly so they caramelise evenly.

Meanwhile, heat a little vegetable oil in a heavy bottomed pressure cooker pan, add the onions and cook over a medium-high heat until heavily caramelised and almost burnt. Remove from the pan and set to one side and repeat this process with the carrots and mushrooms.

Place all of the caramelised ingredients along with the garlic, thyme and peppercorns back into the pan and just cover with cold water. Bring the stock to a simmer and skim any residue that floats on the top whilst heating.

Secure the lid on top and bring to full pressure over a high heat then reduce the heat to low and continue to cook for 45 minutes. Remove from the heat and let it cool enough so the pressure is released, remove the lid and skim any fat from the surface then carefully pass the stock through a fine sieve. Place the stock into a clean heavy based pan and rapidly boil over a high heat until it has reduced by half. Pass through a fine sieve once more then chill and keep in the fridge.

PINE OIL

100g Douglas Fir pine needles, from our neighbouring Pennine forests

100g curly parsley leaves

400g vegetable oil

14g table salt

Blanch the pine needles and parsley leaves in boiling water for 2 minutes then refresh in an ice bath until chilled and squeeze dry and place on to kitchen paper. Place all of the ingredients into a Thermomix and blend on speed 8 for 8 minutes at 60°c and cool over an ice bath immediately. Leave to infuse for 12 hours in a cool dark place then pass through a fine sieve. Keep in the fridge in a dark place until needed.

BERRY COMPOTE

500g berries	
75g fructose (fruit sugar)	
1 vanilla pod, split	
75ml strawberry juice	
1 sprig of thyme	

Place all of the ingredients in a pan and very gently bring to a simmer, cook for five minutes until the liquid has become syrupy and remove from the heat. Cool immediately over an ice bath and keep in the fridge.

GOMME (SUGAR SYRUP)

100ml water, boiling	
200g sugar	

This is sugar syrup added to drinks for extra sweetness and to add body. This can be either bought or made at home. Dissolve 2 parts sugar into 1 part boiling water, stirring constantly. Once completely dissolved remove from heat and allow to cool and thicken.

VEGETABLE STOCK

1kg carrots, peeled and finely sliced

750g white onion, peeled and finely sliced

1.5kg leeks, white parts only, finely sliced

250g celery, finely sliced

500g chestnut mushrooms, finely sliced

3 litres water

15g black peppercorns

5 sprigs of thyme

3 bay leaves

Vegetable oil

Heat a little vegetable oil in a heavy bottomed pressure cooker pan, add the onions and cook over a low heat until softened. Remove from the pan and set to one side, then repeat this process with the rest of the vegetables.

Place all of the caramelised vegetables along with the water, thyme, bay and peppercorns back into the pan and bring the stock to a simmer and skim any residue that floats on the top whilst heating. Secure the lid on top and bring to full pressure over a high heat, then reduce to low and continue to cook for 25 minutes. Remove from the heat and let it cool.

Remove the lid and carefully pass the stock through a fine sieve. Place the stock into a clean heavy based pan and rapidly boil over a high heat until it has reduced by half. Pass through a fine sieve once more then chill and keep in the fridge.

RED ONION MARMALADE

4kg red onions, sliced
6 garlic cloves, thinly sliced
500ml aged balsamic vinegar
30g table salt
5 cloves
10 juniper berries
10g thyme leaves
350g redcurrant jelly
Vegetable Oil

Heat a large heavy based pan and add a little vegetable oil, when hot add the onions and cook over a high heat until they caramelise. Add the garlic and salt and reduce the heat to a low setting.

Wrap the cloves, juniper and thyme in some cheese cloth and tie with string to secure it. Then add it to the pan along with the balsamic vinegar and redcurrant jelly. Simmer over a gentle heat, stirring occasionally until all of the liquid has evaporated.

Remove the cheese cloth parcel and discard it, chill and keep in the fridge until needed.

BEER BATTER

700ml carbonated beer
4 egg whites
680g self raising flour
1 teaspoon bicarbonate of soda
10g table salt

Place the beer, bicarbonate of soda and salt in a large bowl and whisk to combine. Gradually add the flour and whisk until a batter is formed. In a separate bowl whisk the egg whites until frothy and then fold them in to the batter carefully.

PIZZA DOUGH

1kg pizza flour, minimum 12% gluten content

600ml cold water

2g fresh yeast

30g table salt

Place half the flour in a large electric mixing bowl. Combine the yeast and water and whisk them together to dissolve the yeast. Add the liquid to the flour and start to mix on a low speed using the dough hook attachment, until a wet slurry is formed. Add the salt and continue mixing for 2 minutes then add the rest of the flour and mix for 10 minutes, turn off the machine and rest it for 15 minutes.

Turn on the machine and mix again for further 5 minutes.

Place the dough in a large bowl and leave to prove at room temperature for 12 hours.

Knock back the dough and then weigh in to 250g pieces and shape in to balls and place onto a lightly floured tray and cover with cling film and keep in the fridge until needed.

PIZZA SAUCE

550g tinned San Marzano tomatoes

15ml extra virgin olive oil

10g table salt

15g basil leaves

15g oregano leaves

Place all of the ingredients in a tall container and use a stick blender to pulse the mixture to combine. Make sure you don't completely purée it because if you blend too many tomato seeds into the sauce, it will become bitter.

THE MILESTONE
Bar and Restaurant

Discount Voucher

£5 off

THE MILESTONE
Bar and Restaurant

Discount Voucher

£5 off

Discount Voucher

£5 off

Discount Voucher

£5 off

CRAFT & DOUGH

Discount Voucher

£5 off

CRAFT & DOUGH

Discount Voucher

£5 off

Terms & Conditions

THE
MILESTONE
Bar and Restaurant

This voucher is redeemable at The Milestone against a prebooked meal of two people or more. Only one voucher may be used per table booked. Can not be used in conjunction with any other offer. Offer valid until 30/11/2016.

Terms & Conditions

THE
MILESTONE
Bar and Restaurant

This voucher is redeemable at The Milestone against a prebooked meal of two people or more. Only one voucher may be used per table booked. Can not be used in conjunction with any other offer. Offer valid until 30/11/2016.

Terms & Conditions

This voucher is redeemable at The Wig & Pen against a prebooked meal of two people or more. Only one voucher may be used per table booked. Can not be used in conjunction with any other offer. Offer valid until 30/11/2016.

Terms & Conditions

This voucher is redeemable at The Wig & Pen against a prebooked meal of two people or more. Only one voucher may be used per table booked. Can not be used in conjunction with any other offer. Offer valid until 30/11/2016.

Terms & Conditions

CRAFT & DOUGH

This voucher is redeemable at Craft & Dough against a prebooked meal of two people or more. Only one voucher may be used per table booked. Can not be used in conjunction with any other offer. Offer valid until 30/11/2016.

Terms & Conditions

CRAFT & DOUGH

This voucher is redeemable at Craft & Dough against a prebooked meal of two people or more. Only one voucher may be used per table booked. Can not be used in conjunction with any other offer. Offer valid until 30/11/2016.